ALSO BY BARBIE LATZA NADEAU

Roadmap to Hell: Sex, Drugs and Guns on the Mafia Coast

Angel Face: Sex, Murder, and the Inside Story of Amanda Knox

The Godmother

Murder, Vengeance, and the
Bloody Struggle of Mafia Women

BARBIE LATZA NADEAU

 PENGUIN BOOKS

PENGUIN BOOKS
An imprint of Penguin Random House LLC
penguinrandomhouse.com

Copyright © 2022 by Barbie Latza Nadeau
Penguin Random House supports copyright. Copyright fuels creativity,
encourages diverse voices, promotes free speech, and creates a vibrant culture.
Thank you for buying an authorized edition of this book and for complying
with copyright laws by not reproducing, scanning, or distributing any part of
it in any form without permission. You are supporting writers and allowing
Penguin Random House to continue to publish books for every reader.

LIBRARY OF CONGRESS CATALOGING-IN-PUBLICATION DATA
Names: Nadeau, Barbie Latza, author.
Title: The Godmother: murder, vengeance, and the bloody struggle of Mafia
women / Barbie Latza Nadeau.
Description: [New York] : Penguin Books, [2022] |
Includes bibliographical references.
Identifiers: LCCN 2022001193 (print) | LCCN 2022001194 (ebook) |
ISBN 9780143136118 (trade paperback) | ISBN 9780525507727 (ebook)
Subjects: LCSH: Maresca, Pupetta, 1935–2021. |
Women and the mafia—Italy—Biography.
Classification: LCC HV6452.5 .N34 2022 (print) | LCC HV6452.5 (ebook) |
DDC 364.106/6082—dc23/eng/20220118
LC record available at https://lccn.loc.gov/2022001193
LC ebook record available at https://lccn.loc.gov/2022001194

Printed in the United States of America
2nd Printing

Set in Garamond MT Pro
Designed by Sabrina Bowers

Dedicated to my friend and mentor Chris Dickey,
who I wish had lived long enough to read this book he
inspired me to write.

Contents

The Godmother

1

Pupetta's Kitchen

Pupetta claims not to remember pelting Big Tony with what police claim was twenty-nine bullets, insisting that it was just "one or two shots" from the back of the car that she delivered out of fear.

CASTELLAMMARE DI STABIA, Italy—It was a warm summer afternoon and Assunta "Pupetta" Maresca was tapping her manicured jet-black fingernails on a white marble tabletop that was stained with what looked like red wine or blood. We were sitting in the kitchen of her fluorescent-lit apartment in a coastal town of questionable character south of Naples where she was born into a crime family in 1935, and where she died December 29, 2021. The heavy wooden shutters were closed to keep out the heat, and a ceiling lamp swayed in the breeze created by a flimsy plastic fan perched on the counter.

It was months before the COVID pandemic changed the world, and Pupetta's biggest health fear was suffering a stroke, despite doing nothing to prevent it. A pack of menthol cigarettes in a gilded case sat neatly next to an ornate ashtray and matching lighter in the center of the table. A bedazzled vape pen on what looked like a rosary hung on her chest like a necklace. She puffed on it between cigarettes and blew smoke directly into my face. More than once she told me she shouldn't smoke. "These will kill me," she said between puffs. "I should stop."

The crepey skin on the backs of her small hands was too smooth for a woman in her eighties and looked as if it had been surgically stretched around her swollen joints. Her age spots had been bleached and looked like fading bruises, as if someone had clutched her hand too hard. She briefly put her cigarette in the ashtray and picked up a strand of her crimson-dyed hair that had fallen onto the table and stretched it between her fingers, lifting her pinkies ever so slightly before brushing it off to the tile floor for her maid to eventually sweep up.

It was impossible to look at Pupetta's hands without imagining them wrapped around the silver Smith & Wesson .38 pistol she once fired in the defining moment of her life. More than sixty years before I sat with her, she used that gun to take down the man who ordered the fatal hit on her husband. Surely her husband's rival was dead after her first blasts knocked him to the ground. But she still grabbed her thirteen-year-old brother Ciro's revolver and sent another round of bullets—twenty-nine in all—in the direction of the bleeding corpse. The killing took place outside a busy coffee bar in Naples in broad daylight. She was eighteen years old and six months pregnant at the time.

Pupetta claimed she still kept the pistol in the nightstand

next to her bed. I once asked her if I could see it, but she insisted that she would only take it out to use it. I never asked again. Of the many things I grew to admire most about the woman nicknamed Lady Camorra was her dry sense of humor. She was a cunning liar and a cold-blooded killer, but if you could look beyond that, she was genuinely delightful.

The first time I sat in Pupetta's kitchen—after stalking her at her usual coffee bar and vegetable market until she agreed to grant an interview without charging me for it—she offered me bitter espresso served in a chipped demitasse cup, clearly saving the fine china for better company. I stared into the dark, steaming liquid, hesitant to take a sip out of concern that she could have slipped something into it. In a brief bout of egotism, I envisioned that perhaps I could be a last-hurrah killing. No one even knew where I was, and for someone with her connections to the underworld it would be reasonably easy to get rid of my body. Covering crime and murder and death—essentially trafficking in tragedy—for the many years I've been in Italy has jaded my perception of my own mortality. Over the years, I have evolved from thinking that nothing bad will ever happen to me to expecting it. I see the worst first, as I am often reminded by friends and family. I am generally a voice of doom.

In my defense, the paranoia was bolstered by the fact that Pupetta was not drinking any of the espresso herself. Too much caffeine in the afternoon made her nervous, she answered when I asked if she was joining me. I drank it in one gulp, as is the custom in Italy. She watched me closely, enjoying my fear—or at least that's how I choose to remember it. Every time I saw her after that, she also drank coffee with me no matter what time of day.

As we spoke that first afternoon, a radio station played Neapolitan folk songs peppered with advertisements for private home-security services. When the news bulletin came on, she touched her ear to signal me to be quiet so she could listen to see if anyone she knows had been caught up in something unseemly.

Pupetta was wearing a dark purple tank top that pushed her enormous soft breasts together to create wrinkly, freckled cleavage over which the vape pen perilously dangled, at times threatening to fall inside. She was sitting on a squeaky wooden chair on a faded Thulian pink floral pillow that made her seem much taller than she is. Every time she fidgeted, the chair let out a tired groan, prompting the old French bulldog sleeping at her feet to growl in his sleep.

Everything that was not covered in plastic in Pupetta's adjacent living room was instead draped with crocheted lace doilies. Pretty hand-painted blue-and-yellow plates from Sicily hung on the walls and elegantly framed pictures of her twins at various stages of their lives were lined up on a polished chest of drawers against the dining room wall. There were no pictures of her first son, Pasqualino, to whom she gave birth in prison while serving a sentence for murder and who mysteriously disappeared when he was eighteen years old.

Outside the window, the beaches of Pupetta's hometown are littered with fuel canisters and discarded fishing gear washed in from the polluted Mediterranean Sea. Signs warn swimmers to avoid the water, but there are at least half a dozen elderly men digging for clams out there on any day of the year. In the winter, they wear thigh-high waders and heavy jackets. In the summer, they're in brightly colored Speedos and flip-flops. The seafront town has one of the clearest views anywhere of the full breadth of Mount Vesuvius, the volcano that destroyed the original town of nearby Stabiae during its infamous AD 79 eruption.

Castellammare di Stabia sprung from those ashes and is synonymous with moral decay—so much so that in 2015 a local priest performed an exorcism by helicopter, symbolically spraying out gallons of holy water high above the 65,000 inhabitants to make sure he didn't miss a single sinful soul. Crime didn't stop, though the aerial blessing did miraculously make the town's calcium-clogged fountains spring back to life, or so the legend goes. The Neapolitan Camorra's criminal roots run too deep here for a clerical cleansing, and Pupetta is emblematic of all that is wrong about this crime-ridden backwater.

The first time I stayed in Castellammare, I rented a rooftop Airbnb that gave me clear views of the city, sea, and menacing volcano. The woman who let it to me wanted to be clear that I understood that I wasn't on the Amalfi Coast, the tony luxury resort area just across the Sorrentine Peninsula where organized crime is relegated to the background, not as blatantly out front as it is in Castellammare. Though the town is no more than half an hour from splendorous Sorrento itself, Castellammare is simply another world—a sinister one where criminality has permeated every corner of society. When I explained that I was a journalist chasing a mafia-related story, she seemed relieved. She wouldn't have to apologize for the rampant delinquency of the city that was easily witnessed from her terrace. At any given time of the day or night, people were huddled together on the streets below, trading in any manner of contraband. During the many times I visited, I saw little bags of drugs being handed over for cash and from the rooftop terrace a large box that could have easily held a substantial weapon. The nervous seller seemed ready to get rid of it and the buyer ran immediately to a waiting BMW with dark windows and sped away.

Every time I left the apartment, I felt like I was being watched. The streets of Castellammare are lined with normal-seeming shops, but on close observation they seemed like fronts for other businesses. No one ever appeared to be carrying a bag as they walked out, not even as they were still standing at the cash register. People gave strange nods to each other, almost as if there were lookouts posted on corners. Expensive cars were as prominent as rusted Fiats, and the harbor was lined with extravagant yachts even though the average reported income in this town hovers slightly above the poverty line. I visited many times, but could never quite figure out the heart and soul of the city. Perhaps because it didn't have one. The pet shops sell small mice to feed pythons and other exotic reptiles that are popular among residents for reasons that don't seem entirely clear. The lingerie shops have whole sections of red apparel, samples of which find their way into window displays even when it's not Valentine's Day—an exhibition that long perplexed me.

It is hard to explain why the mafia is still so powerful in this country, a wealthy nation that often trips over its bureaucracy and gets tangled up in its laborious judicial system. The mafia exists not in spite of this country, but so many of the country's failings have been created by the enduring existence of organized crime. Like other terrorist organizations, including many who use Italy's organized crime syndicates to enter Europe illegally or rely on them for fake documents or weapons, the mafia derives its strength from a combination of fear and complacency. It is so often said that the mafia is part of Italy's DNA, and while anti-mafia forces have done a great deal to fight the three main groups—the Cosa Nostra (Our Thing) in Sicily, the 'Ndrangheta in Calabria, and the Neapolitan Camorra in Campania—historically speaking, the only real Mafia is the Sicilian Cosa Nostra (the historical American Mafia families are all tied to Sicily, though the Camorra and 'Ndrangheta have more recently spread across Europe and the Americas, too).

Despite the Cosa Nostra being the original and most well-known of the major Italian organizations, the Italian criminal-justice system refers to crimes committed by other known groups as "mafia-related" under its law Article 41-bis, which was developed specifically to aid Italian law enforcement in the fight against organized crime. In 2018, the term Mafia Capitale, or Capital Mafia, was christened, used to describe the local mafia-style group in Rome. Italy also recognizes several Nigerian mafia-style groups and have charged their members with "mafia" crimes.

To truly understand Italy's organized-crime culture—if that is possible, given its secrecy and the fact that what we know about these organizations comes mostly from those who betray them and have an ax to grind with them—you need to understand how the culture has been allowed to prosper here for so long. Anti-mafia prosecutor Alessandra Cerreti is the only person who has ever explained the continuation of the mafia's influence on this country to me in a way that truly made sense.

The mafia—in the most general meaning of the term, encompassing all of the organized crime groups in Italy—is what she calls a "parallel state" and remains to this day "politically protected" because of the success these groups have had infiltrating every layer of Italian life. They have allies and fellow mobsters in every sector, from the highest levels of government on down to the city-park gardeners who prove useful when it comes to finding places to hide drugs or relay overheard conversations. These men and women don't act like petty criminals who might nab a wallet from a tourist on the Amalfi Coast or steal gas in some backwater in Sicily; they are indistinguishable from law-abiding citizens, often working as civil servants who should have been—and maybe were—vetted. Full city councils have been dissolved to purge local government of deep infiltrations. But mafiosi normally act more like spies than infiltrators, relaying information that could be useful to exploit, or fixing contracts and bids to make sure they go to mob-tied companies.

Almost like schools of fish, the criminal groups are large but agile enough to escape or hunt depending on the circumstances. Their strength is not just in numbers, but in the fact that they are more represented in the top echelons of power than any force trying to defeat them. "It is not surreal," Cerreti says. "They operate in the real world."

And that real world is everywhere in Italy. Pupetta's father was not a top boss, but a notable criminal gang leader whose territory included Castellammare di Stabia and the neighboring hamlets that dot the winding roads between the tourist haven of Sorrento, overlooking the stunning Amalfi Coast to the south and the gritty backstreets of Naples to the north. He was a known and respected criminal among his peers, specializing in contraband cigarettes, which was a lucrative enterprise in postwar Italy.

The Maresca family clansmen were known as Lampetielli, or lightning strikes, named so for the deadly efficiency of their signature switchblades, used in equal parts to threaten and kill.[1] As happens to be the case, Pupetta's first trouble with the law came in primary school, when she knifed the daughter of another local criminal. The charges were dropped when the victim suddenly refused to testify. When I asked her about it, she called the whole incident "blown up" and merely a childhood spat, despite the fact that she knew how to wield a weapon before she had her first menstrual period.

Pupetta's four brothers tried to protect her honor and keep her away from the untoward advances of suitors who approached with something other than honorable intentions. It proved a daunting task. From a very young age, Pupetta knew how to exploit her beauty for whatever she wanted, and she continued to try to do so long after it had faded.

At its rawest, most nubile, she used her attractiveness, confirmed by a local pageant title, to lure emerging Camorra boss Pasquale "Pasqualone" Simonetti. Pasqualone 'e Nola—Big Pasquale as everyone called him—was a mountain of a man with wiry black hair and a round chin that melted into his thick stubbled neck. At more than six feet tall, he towered over his "little doll," from which the nickname Pupetta derives. Italians often use the suffix -*one* to describe things that are larger than normal. Christmas dinner is not a *cena* but a *cenone*, and a big kiss is not a *bacio* but a *bacione*. Pasqualone fit the customary use perfectly.

He was a classic Camorra underboss—wealthy, well dressed, and ruthless. He commanded respect through the usual tenets of the criminal underworld: extortion, coercion, and casual murder. Before Pupetta came into his life, Pasqualone was called the presidente dei prezzi, "president of prices." He lorded over the Camorra's vegetable and greengrocery racket in the heart of the bountiful Neapolitan farmland, which at the time produced about a quarter of a million dollars in annual profits (around US $2.2 million in today's money), from tomatoes, zucchini, potatoes, peaches, and lemons.

That was long before the Camorra destroyed the trade by burying toxic waste on the flanks of Mount Vesuvius, causing dioxin levels to spike and making the tomatoes unfit for export, though they were still eaten locally. To this day, the levels soar every few years and the buffalo milk that has made the local mozzarella so famous becomes too toxic to export. The triangle of land around the volcano, which has come to be referred to as the terra dei fuochi, "land of fires,"[2] due to the number of rogue blazes set by the Camorra to burn toxic waste in the mid-2000s, is emblematic of the ways in which crime has so deeply destroyed so much of this otherwise exceptional country. On a reporting trip to cover the toxic fires just a few years after I arrived in Rome, I was taken aback by the grime stuck to my car. Only days later when I started coughing up black phlegm did I stop to think that in covering a story about thick black smoke, I would have to breathe it myself.

We journalists in general tend to think of ourselves as being immune, heading toward the flames of the latest disaster like naive moths assuming we won't get burned. From earthquakes to murder scenes, our gallows humor forms a sort of shield against thinking too much about the reality of what we know we will never unsee. In Italy, journalists like Roberto Saviano and Federica Angeli live with round-the-clock police protection for writing about the mafia. Saviano's bestselling book *Gomorrah* won him a life sentence for writing about the Camorra where he grew up near Naples, and Angeli lives under constant threat for her work uncovering the Roman Casamonica mafia. Countless other journalists who cover mafia crimes are at risk just investigating stories and going to crime scenes, where they could be seen as a threat or get caught in cross fire. Journalists who name names or untangle intricate ties between businesses and crime groups are especially vulnerable. Many are just threatened at first, with a bullet sent to their house or some other unmistakable sign, like their pets being killed or a note left inside their apartment. The message is clear: this time is a warning, next time we'll kill you unless you stop.

The Italian environmental group Legambiente has for years warned of an environmental apocalypse in the terra dei fuochi, which, coupled with the endemic corruption often driven by organized crime that has crippled the health care system, makes the damage done here especially daunting. Childhood cancer levels are the highest in the European Union. More than

100,000 tons of toxic waste, much of it shipped in from all over Europe, have been dumped, buried, and burned on the slopes of the still very active volcano, thanks to the Camorra's enterprising garbage division that charges far less than legitimate companies to dispose of toxic waste. Authorities were able to trace the use of 400,000 semitrucks that ferried the waste from 443 companies across Europe, many of which were later sanctioned, though not enough to stop the practice.

After the bombs of World War II ravaged much of southern Italy, farmers had no choice but to pay protection money and adhere to prices set by underbosses like Pasqualone if they wanted to eke out a living. If they didn't? At best, they would watch their barns burn down. At worst, they would be buried alive beneath their crops. Outside producers who tried to break into the market to buy directly from the farmers were met with hefty fees—also levied by the various underbosses like Pasqualone. Or they were chased away—often with gunfire—which kept farmers dependent on the mob if they wanted to sell their crops.

After the war, many southern Italians struggled to lift themselves out of debilitating poverty, which made easy work for organized-crime groups that hid behind a Robin Hood–style facade. History is repeating itself following Italy's plunge into recession as a result of the COVID pandemic. This was especially true during the second wave, which brought the area around Naples to its knees and pushed people who had until then resisted the mob's help to realize the state had failed and they couldn't survive without the Camorra.

Just as after the war, many small businesses in this part of

Italy didn't qualify for government aid—for the most part because they evaded taxes and underreported their incomes to such an extent the government aid to replace their legal income came nowhere near their real turnover. And without enough legally recognized collateral for bank loans, they had no choice but to turn to organized-crime syndicates to rescue them. That's how the various mafias survive. People like Pasqualone and those following in his footsteps act as "goodwill" ambassadors who help "the little guy" when the state fails them, as it often does, and keep the criminal cycle—and the local population—alive.

Pasqualone bolstered the local farmers during those tough years, solving people's problems in exchange for any number of paybacks, including complicity in his criminal enterprise. He doled out favors to anyone who might have something to offer in return, from an empty outbuilding to store stolen goods to an alibi if he might one day need it. He famously helped the errantly pregnant daughter of a foot soldier in his organization after her boyfriend refused to commit. Pasqualone told him that he had around $100,000 that the young punk could choose how to spend: on his wedding or on his funeral.[3]

Pasqualone also dabbled in the lucrative contraband cigarette distribution enterprise that grew out of postwar rationing. US and British soldiers stationed in Naples had fed a booming black market in American smokes. When the war ended and the Allies went home, the cigarette supply stopped coming in, but by then the Italians were hooked. The state stepped in to ration foreign-made cigarettes entering the country through southern Italian ports, which opened up an obvious business opportunity for any crime boss who could smuggle in enough to feed the demand.

For a Camorra guappo like Pasqualone, working around the state's rules and bringing the contraband in directly from overseas made for easy money despite the intense competition to control the trade. Dominance in organized crime is often achieved through bloodshed and, in 1952, Pasqualone was sentenced to eight years in prison for the attempted murder of Alfredo Maisto, an associate-turned-rival who had started edging into his cigarette territory.

As soon as Pasqualone was behind bars, another close associate, Antonio Esposito, known as Totonno 'e Pomigliano, or Big Tony, took over his share of the vegetable price racket, promising Pasqualone a cut while he was in the can. At first, he funneled some of the profits to Pasqualone behind bars, but within a few months he was keeping everything for himself.

In 1954, just two years into his eight-year sentence, Pasqualone was suddenly released from prison after new evidence emerged in the attempted murder charge—or, more likely, after a judge was threatened or paid off. Naturally, he wanted his old turf back and soon he picked up right where he'd left off. Just as predictably, Big Tony had no intention of giving up the new territory. But Pasqualone was too preoccupied with other matters to notice the tension brewing.

If two years in jail had taught Pasqualone anything, it was that he didn't want to be alone. He watched how his fellow inmates' wives and lovers enriched their idle time, and he wanted someone to dote on him as well. He had met Pupetta shortly before he went into prison. She caught his eye after she won a local beauty pageant and he decided she would be his bride.

He was as equally impressed by her beauty as her criminal pedigree from the Lampetielli clan's line of work. Once in prison, he encouraged her love letters with lofty responses and promises of a life together. Within days of his release, Pasqualone started courting her seriously, and Pupetta's brothers—who had previously prohibited her from dating any other clansmen—stepped out of the way and quickly approved of her new suitor, knowing that someone of Pasqualone's ranking would boost their own.

Pupetta and Pasqualone were married on April 27, 1955, when she was just seventeen years old. More than five hundred guests filled the church for the lavish Catholic wedding, including the influential dons of the Camorra clans who showered them with jewelry and envelopes stuffed with cash.[4] Even those with whom Pasqualone had sparred over territory, like Big Tony, and a gun-for-hire named Gaetano Orlando, whose nickname was Tanino 'e Bastimento, attended to celebrate the union of two important criminal lineages. Everything was perfect, and though their life together would never be easy, it seemed destined for blissful longevity.

They set about making their new home, and Pupetta said she was determined after they got married that they would leave their life of crime and do something less risky. It is questionable whether that was ever possible, and of course in retrospect it is an easy claim to make. The reality is that it would have been too hard for them to leave that life. They had no employable skills, and criminal associations and reputations that would have made any potential employer nervous. And anyway, those born into such strong criminal families rarely leave that world alive.

Just months after their future together seemed sealed, on a blistering humid day in mid-July, Pasqualone lay slowly bleeding to death from gunshots to the gut following an attack carried out in Naples' steamy central market square during the busiest time of the morning. Pasqualone was at the market to collect protection money and distribute favors among the farmers under his control. He was shot while peeling an orange handed to him by one of them, which has caused some speculation that the offer of fruit was meant as a distraction and that the shooter did not act alone.

The square, lined with basilicas that include the ornate Santa Croce e Purgatorio, where elderly women still gather every day to pray for the souls of the dead who are stuck in purgatory, was packed when the shots were fired. But the only person who ever said they saw who pulled the trigger was Pasqualone himself.

A newly pregnant Pupetta was called to the emergency room and wept at his bedside for the nearly twelve hours he lingered until he died at dawn, sending her shattered dreams to his grave with him. Between his last breaths, Pasqualone told his young wife that the shooter was Gaetano Orlando, one of their wedding attendees. He also told her Orlando was sent by Big Tony, the rival who tried to cut him out of the vegetable-market racket while he was in prison.

A few days later, Pupetta buried her beloved, whom she referred to as her Prince Charming or Principe Azzurro until the day she died. She vowed upon his grave to avenge his death, even though it was unheard of at the time for a woman to make such a claim. "Those days were long and lonely," she told me as she paged through the faded black-and-white photographs and newspaper society-page clippings plastered in her crumbling wedding album. "I was at a point where I could just fade away or make things right. I decided I had no choice but to make things right."

Pupetta always blamed the police, saying they left her no choice but to take justice into her own hands. Even as an eighteen-year-old pregnant mob widow and clansman's daughter, she'd had enough faith in the rule of law to believe the authorities would help her. But the clear lack of urgency by the police to hold someone accountable for her husband's broad-daylight murder forced her to rely on her own methods over the state's.

Pupetta said she told police that Big Tony ordered the hit on Pasqualone and that Orlando pulled the trigger. Orlando was eventually arrested and sent to prison, but prosecutors chose not to act on Big Tony's role. "I gave his name to the police but they said they needed proof to arrest him," she told me, though the police records from that time tell a slightly different story in that she gave a different name than Big Tony's, clearly hoping they would arrest someone else as a warning that he would be next. "What they really meant was that they didn't have the balls to get involved or that they owed him protection."

Big Tony was keenly aware that the death of such an up-and-coming guappo like Pasqualone would be avenged. So he threatened Pupetta, playing manipulative games like leaving messages in places where he knew she would be to catch her off guard. It was his attempt to scare her—warning her that if she did anything, she and her unborn baby would disappear without a trace. Still, Big Tony knew well the rules under which they all lived, especially the most important: leaving a murder such as Pasqualone's unavenged was out of the question. But his biggest mistake was underestimating the young widow and discounting the possibility that she would carry out the act of revenge herself.

Pupetta remembered vividly the day of Pasqualone's funeral. It was that day when she decided that she would be no fool or vehicle to elevate Big Tony's position in the ranks. "I took Pasqualone's gun from his nightstand and carried it with me from the day I buried him until the day I used it," she says. She never once doubted that she could do it. As the children of a clansman, she and her brothers had all learned how to shoot a gun to defend themselves. Their father made sure of it. "He taught me to shoot and made sure that I could hit any target between the eyes," she explained, recounting the story of her loving father teaching her to shoot in the same way someone else might recall a parent helping their child learn to play a musical instrument or swing a baseball bat. "I was a good shot from the first time I picked up a piece, and I made him proud."

Nearly three months after Pasqualone was laid to rest, Pupetta, by then bulging in her final trimester of pregnancy, finally got to use the weapon. When I asked her to describe Pasqualone's gun, she pretended to point the imaginary firearm vaguely toward my forehead. "It was a petite gun," she said, pulling the air trigger as she made a clicking sound with her tongue. "It was the kind you carry in a little clutch purse like you'd take out to a nice dinner."

On the day that would set the course of Pupetta's life, she

had asked her thirteen-year-old brother, Ciro, to come with her to the cemetery to lay flowers on Pasqualone's tomb, as remains the custom for new widows in this part of Italy for a year after a husband's death. Their driver, Nicola Vistocco, was also going to stop by the market square where Pasqualone was killed so Pupetta could pick up some produce, which was given to her for free.

On the way to the market, she spotted Big Tony coming out of a busy coffee bar on the Corso Novara, not far from the square where her husband was shot. She asked Nicola to pull her Fiat over, and he slouched low behind the steering wheel while Pupetta waited. Once Big Tony was walking down the Corso Novara, she asked Nicola to drive up to him. Nicola stopped the car and Pupetta jumped out and started shooting, a gunfight ensued and Pupetta, protected by the car, easily escaped any harm. The driver didn't see a thing, he told police. He and Ciro were both later tried and convicted for acting as accessories to murder.

Pupetta initially claimed that he had tried to open the car door and she pulled her gun only in self-defense. She claims not to remember pelting Big Tony with what police claim were twenty-nine bullets, insisting that it was just "one or two shots" from the back of the car delivered out of fear. But the evidence used to convict her—including gruesome autopsy photos—showed she used Pasqualone's Smith & Wesson with precision, and then used the revolver carried by her little brother to make sure he was properly dead. Five of the bullets went straight into her husband's assassin's skull. Some reports suggest that four guns were used, which would help explain the astonishing

number of bullets. It would also imply greater Camorra involvement and an organized vendetta. When I asked, Pupetta
brushed that off and insisted that the reports don't take into account that the area where the murder took place was already
littered with shell casings and the walls were scarred from previous gun battles.

The two siblings fled the scene, leaving the crimson chrysanthemums meant for Pasqualone's grave in the back seat.
When Pupetta died, I bought chrysanthemums in the same
color as she described to place on the family tomb where she
was interred, though police wouldn't allow me to do so, as any
nonfamily celebration of her life was prohibited. After a few
weeks in hiding, Pupetta was ratted out and arrested for Big
Tony's murder. It seemed especially telling to her that she was
so easily brought to justice after all she went through to try to
get the police to find anyone responsible for her husband's murder. The fact that they did not turn the same blind eye to Big
Tony's killing convinced her that either his clan controlled the
local investigators or that he was an informant.

During her murder trial, she showed no remorse at all, instead telling the court that she would "do it again" if she had
the chance. It was her duty to avenge her husband's death in the
absence of the law, she said, screaming during one hearing, "I
killed for love!" before collapsing in the courtroom.[6] Local
newspapers covered the trial like it was a social event. Headlines screamed about Pupetta's many outbursts in court,[7] often
paying the same attention to detail in describing how the youthful defendant dressed and batted her long eyelashes as

newspapers normally paid to starlets of her generation like Sophia Loren, a contemporary who also grew up in the area.

The prosecutor in the case said that by acting to avenge her husband's death—essentially playing judge, jury, and executioner for a crime never tried in court—she was participating in what they called an "episode of gang warfare"[8] and argued for a life sentence. Her lawyer argued first that it was a crime of self-defense, an argument that Pupetta had promptly undermined on the very first day she testified with her outburst about killing for love. He then changed tack to try to defend the case as a diletto per amore, or an "honor crime," which covered a broad category of offenses that could somehow be justified by heartbreak. Crimes to defend one's honor were so common in Italy they were even considered an extenuating circumstance in sentencing until the 1990s, when it finally became more difficult, though even today not impossible, for a cuckolded husband to kill a cheating wife[9] or a mafioso avenging murder to get a pass.

The trial, which also included the side attraction of Pasqualone's hit man Gaetano Orlando's case, was open to the public, and a number of Big Tony's associates were present in the gallery to make sure that the omertà, or code of silence that extends across all of Italy's criminal enterprises, was properly respected. Of the eighty-five witnesses called, very few said they saw anything, knew anything, or would speak of anything relevant to the court's final deliberation.

Fulfilling the vendetta served a second by-product—and one that Pupetta never could have imagined. The act lifted her to icon status among the Neapolitan criminal elite, earning her the nickname Lady Camorra and giving her incomparable stature as an original madrina—a godmother. After just one appearance in court, local Camorristi started throwing flowers onto her police van roof as it traveled between the jail and tribunal, as if she were royalty passing by in a horse-drawn carriage.

Pupetta was quickly found guilty and sentenced to twenty-four years in prison, which was reduced on appeal to thirteen years and four months. She served less than ten years, winning a suspicious pardon in 1965 that likely grew from a deal brokered for information. She dismissed that wholeheartedly when I asked her, insisting that new evidence against Big Tony proved that she had indeed justifiably killed her husband's assassin, and that the judge finally saw the light. Even though I had been told by an assistant to the prosecutor who helped secure her release that a deal had been cut, it made more sense not to confront her with the truth. This is a woman who has time and again shown very little respect for what Italians call the verita.

Her brother Ciro was sentenced to twelve years for his complicity, but acquitted on appeal. Rumors swirled that he had also cut a deal, handing over information about some underling who could be sacrificed to secure a shorter sentence.

The last time I interviewed her, Pupetta smiled when I called her Lady Camorra, though she wouldn't admit she once loved the nickname so much she had the term in Italian embroidered on a throw pillow. She spoke cautiously about the years between when she was released from prison and the

1980s, when she is believed to have wielded tremendous power in her local clan.

She spoke even less candidly about the years after that. She cringed when I asked her to explain how it was that she was investigated for ordering the revenge murder of Ciro Galli, a henchman for one of her archenemies, in 1981 and investigated once more in 1985 for the beheading of criminologist and forensic psychiatrist Aldo Semerari. She was acquitted in both cases, which she said is all that needs to be discussed on either matter.

I asked Pupetta how she hoped to be remembered one day, to which she told me, "Not for these outrageous crimes." Instead, she wanted to be remembered "as an honest woman and loving mother and grandmother." As fate would have it, she was only remembered for the vendetta against her husband's killer.

Felia Allum, a PhD and notable author and organized-crime expert who lectures at England's University of Bath, has doubts that Pupetta wielded any power after the 1980s. She explained to me that misrepresentation of women in the mafia is most likely because the history of the mafia is almost always written by men who use Italy's patriarchal society as the unquestionable guiding light of the country's gender dynamics. Women in noncriminal Italian society are victims of the same circumstances, often overlooked or undervalued as if it's not possible a female could be a CEO or top strategist without having slept her way into the position, or being born into a family determined to give it to her. In the Camorra especially, where Pupetta thrived, women are making far more progress climbing the ladder and being treated as equals than their law-abiding peers. As Allum says, "in many ways, women in organized crime have reached higher levels sooner than women in Italian society."

Having spent the better part of twenty-five years in Italy myself, I can see how the record is often skewed by Italy's patriarchal context. Just as happens with nauseating frequency in Italy's regular society, women tied to mafia organizations aren't often thought to be smart enough to be in charge. In the case of mafia women, for years they were rarely taken seriously in judicial circumstances, even when their names were on deeds or their fingerprints on the smoking gun. That meant they got away with murder—often literally.

Murders aside, Allum has doubts that Pupetta was as bad as she liked people to believe. Still, in 2019, police found a tranche of handwritten notes and letters she wrote to Adolfo Greco as recently as 2018, a clan boss who was charged with extortion and aggravated mafia collusion for his direct involvement in four Camorra clans. An investigation in 2021 into the financial dealings of Ciro Giordano, aka Ciruzzo 'a Varchetella found that between 1987 and 2001, a number of people from competing clans were on the same payroll. An investigator says they found "multiple checks" of large sums of old Italian lire written to Pupetta, among others. Italy switched to the single European currency in 2002, meaning all financial records would have become easier to hide. This could perhaps explain why signs of the payouts ended abruptly and yet none of the former recipients seemed to show any sign that they had suffered a loss of income.

Greco, who was one of a number of mafia thugs released from prison and put on house arrest[10] during the coronavirus pandemic, allegedly orchestrated a regional network of corrupt officials in the local government of Castellammare di Stabia and the local entities. When he was arrested, police said they found Rolexes and suitcases full of hundred-euro notes alongside Pupetta's letters. "The pentiti have ruined me," she wrote in one, referring to former mafiosi who turn state's witnesses. "Please give my son a position."

What's most remarkable about that letter, which was presented in court during Greco's mafia collusion trial in late 2019, is the familiarity and tone. Greco was clearly more than a little-known power broker she was asking about legitimate work for her son. If anyone could have helped her find her son work within the local Camorra circuit, it would have been Adolfo Greco—and it is clear that her familiarity with the secret hierarchy would have only come from people within the criminal realm.

In 2020, as the pandemic ravaged Italy, Pupetta said to me that her lawyer advised her to no longer speak to anyone without him—even as every lawyer whose name she gave me told me he no longer represented her—implying she was under scrutiny once again. It was then that her daughter, Antonella, very much her mother's gatekeeper, expressed her first hint of displeasure that Pupetta was talking to a journalist, and without some guarantee of financial or other reward.

I asked the anti-mafia prosecutor Alessandra Cerreti for her thoughts on Pupetta's infamy.

"She has created much of it herself," she replied. Cerreti has dealt with enough bad women to know who is real and who is not, and added that there were many women in Italy with a bloodier track record than Pupetta. I would soon learn exactly what she meant. Pupetta was certainly the first, but by no means was she the worst.

2

Crime School /
Naples' Notorious Prison

"You have grandmothers, daughters, granddaughters of the same family coming through for the same crimes, all tied to the Camorra," she said. Like correctional facilities anywhere in the world, life on the inside is often more corrupt than outside.

Pupetta gave birth to Pasqualino, or little Pasquale, while she was in what was then the women's section of the notorious Poggioreale prison in central Naples. The women's section closed decades ago, and the prison is now, as it was then, described as the worst correctional facility in Italy. The prison, built for just 1,600, has around 2,300 prisoners crammed into various pavilions named after beautiful Italian cities. Many of the cells have cooking facilities that amount to gas burners and a sink, which means the inmates have to cook for themselves rather than being fed in a cafeteria. The cells are jammed with as many as fifteen inmates in dank spaces built for ten, and a constant smell of sewage from backed-up toilets wafts through the humid air.

Over the years, Poggioreale has earned its nickname "crime school," a place where people come out much more deviant than they went in. The prison is ringed by a brown stone wall and was in March 2020 the site of a fiery prison riot, when the coronavirus lockdown led to the restriction of visitors. The riot had actually begun outside the gates, started by women protesting when they were prohibited from visiting their men and bringing them their weekly supply of home-cooked meals—and undoubtedly outside information to the many mafiosi locked inside.

A court case in 2019 unveiled the horrors that took place in Poggioreale's "cell zero," where prisoners were beaten—sometimes to death—or tortured for what was alleged to be the guards' pleasure. Pietro Ioia, an ex-Camorra clansman who now runs an organization called ex-DON for former Camorra detainees, showed me his scars from his time in cell zero when we first met in late 2019.

He wrote a book and screenplay and acted in a local theater production that ran in Naples and Rome, each about the torture. His book, *La Cella Zero: Morte e Rinascita di un Uomo in Gabbia* (*Cell Zero: Death and Rebirth of a Man in a Cage*), which is a favorite among Camorra members, led to a court case against a dozen prison guards; proceedings have been sidelined by the pandemic. I first met Pietro at a dank café during a torrential rainstorm outside the Poggioreale prison in 2019 while he was waiting for a prisoner jailed for affiliation with the Neapolitan Camorra to be released. We could barely hear each other over the sound of the rain pelting the plastic tent that covered the outdoor seating area on the sidewalk, which quickly flooded due to the blocked gutters, leaving our feet soaked.

He had brought with him a woman named "Maria" who dealt with female prisoners. In my years in Italy, I have come to be suspicious of anyone named Maria who doesn't give her last name, which was the case with this Maria. She explained the various ways in which I could essentially embed with women who were being released following imprisonment for Camorra-related crimes. All my options involved some sort of payment. Eventually, we agreed that I could hire one of the women as a "fixer" to guide me into this particular underworld, much the same way I would hire someone in Greece, for example, to help set up interviews and translate while chasing a story. I explained that I would give a fiscal receipt and she could determine whether to claim it for her taxes or not, knowing fully that she never would.

Pietro painted a vivid picture of the Neapolitan prison system, explaining that his scars had come from the guards torturing him after being convicted of drug crimes related to the Camorra. He explained that the guards often used wet towels to whip inmates and made them flex their muscles before they struck so the bruises were deeper. Pietro says they stripped the prisoners down and used sharp objects and ropes to carry out hours of torture before leaving them to whimper alone in the cold, dark cell for days on end, often writhing in pain amid their own blood and urine in an area of the prison where there were no CCTV cameras. There was a time early in my career in Italy when I would have flinched at his descriptions, taking them at face value. But as he spoke, I couldn't help but try to instead weigh how truthful he was and to what extent he was embellishing the details to try to embarrass the state.

The "crime school" has a reputation for turning even light offenders into hardened criminals, and as a place where drugs and sex are usually easy to come by. Many inmates who have been released say it's easy to buy cocaine and other drugs that are delivered to the cells by corrupt guards for the right price. It is also easy to pay to be taken to a room where a prostitute will happily give a blow job for a few euros. That the story is repeated countless times, of course, does not prove it is true— nor does it prove that it is not.

Poggioreale prison no longer has a women's section; the Casa Circondariale Femminile in the seaside town of Pozzuoli is where many of the Camorra women now end up. The female lineages of entire families pass through that prison, an administrator told me. "You have grandmothers, daughters, granddaughters of the same family coming through for the same crimes, all tied to the Camorra," she said. Like hardened correctional facilities anywhere in the world, life on the inside is often more corrupt than outside.

In late 2019, by way of a series of contacts, Maria introduced me to several women in their early thirties who had each just been released from different women's prisons. All had served around ten years for drug smuggling and other crimes tied to Camorra activities. Italy has five dedicated women's prisons: Pozzuoli near Naples, Trani in Puglia, Rebibbia in Rome, Empoli near Florence, and Giudecca in Venice, each notorious for

reasons of their own. Several other prisons have "female sections," especially in sparsely populated areas.

As agreed with Maria, I talked to one of the ex-cons, whom
we'll call "Carmela," about working as my fixer—I would need
her to translate not just the language for me but the context in
which the stories I'd hear took place. As an added bonus—at
least as far as I was concerned—she would protect me, even
though she was a petite woman much smaller than I am. I offered her what I would pay any fixer in similar circumstances,
and after a tough negotiation, she agreed after I showed her
emails and receipts of fixers I had hired elsewhere.

A few days after we agreed on a price, she gave me a date and
time along with an address in the crime-ridden Spanish Quarter of Naples. She told me not to wear any flashy jewelry or
expensive-looking clothes, and to just walk up the central stair-
case to the top floor and knock. Just don't use the elevator, she
advised. The building was recent by Italian standards, likely
constructed in the 1950s when post–World War II money and
the fall of Benito Mussolini had fed the coffers of the Camorra.
Concrete patchwork on the outside of the building spoke to any
number of maintenance issues. Loose wires hung like clotheslines between the building and the one nearby, likely carrying
electricity from a paying customer to those inside.

Out of an abundance of what I thought at the time was
caution but was actually stupidity, I left everything but a phone,
a little cash, and an unmarked envelope containing her payment. I had even swapped my usual iPhone for an older model
I keep on hand for reporting on natural disasters and other

assignments where a nice phone might get damaged. Everything else stayed behind in my hotel room, meaning I went to the appointment without any identification at all. In retrospect, that was probably not smart. Had there been a drug bust while I was in the apartment, it would have been convenient to have an ID to be able to prove who I was.

The faint sound of radios or televisions—it was hard to tell the difference—provided the only hint of life behind the closed doors that marked each floor of the dusty, rundown building. The echo of my footsteps on the cold marble stairs triggered an angry dog that started howling and scratching as I passed by a dark door on one floor and heard what sounded like the flutter of birds from behind another door on the next floor up. I thought I could feel wary eyes looking out behind peepholes the higher I ascended, as if the animals had served as a warning that a stranger was in the building. On the way up, it struck me that I probably should have given someone the address for where I was meeting Carmela, but it seemed like it might raise an unnecessary alarm to send it now from the stairwell.

In these many years of covering stories like this, it had become easier not to tell any nonjournalist friends what I was doing because they often thought I was foolish for taking risks. And telling another journalist you are going somewhere dangerous was like preaching to the choir and garnered little concern. So no one knew where I was and, in fact, neither did I.

The landing on the fifth and final floor led out to the building's flat rooftop. To my immediate right, I could see a doorway under a corrugated plastic sheet, darkened by a thick layer of bird shit, that was balancing on two walls to create a little awning. Farther along the rooftop was what appeared to be an old rusting shipping container (there was a port nearby). Its windowless door looked about two inches taller than the opening it was meant to cover. The container had been for some reason hoisted on top of the building, likely long after the original structure was completed, or perhaps left there during construction.

Across the wide expanse of the rooftop was a twisted labyrinth of clotheslines, water pipes, and tangled cables from satellite dishes and TV antennas, but no other doors that I could see. Graffiti was scribbled all along the low brick wall that lined the edge but would not have kept anyone from falling—or being pushed—over. Blackened spots from fires scarred the tile floor.

I walked to the shipping container and knocked once on its oversized door. After a few minutes of muffled voices that sounded like a hushed argument coming from inside, a little girl dressed in a pretty pink tracksuit who couldn't have been more than five years old opened the door. She said nothing as she turned to go back inside, so I followed her into the shipping container and closed the door behind me. She led me down a short hallway that opened to a dark sitting room on the left that looked like it had been added on to the container, and a brightly lit kitchen on the right that was decorated in Americana country kitsch. The walls were covered with peeling blue calico print wallpaper. White cotton curtains tied back with pretty bows revealed windows cut out of the old shipping crate. Every few feet, appliqués of chickens and roosters were plastered onto the surfaces.

The counters were lined with containers in the shape of chickens. The big ones were labeled for flour and smaller ones for sugar. The dish towels all had the same poultry motif. There were wooden signs with "Welcome" and "Kitchen" in English, like you might see in a house where I grew up in South Dakota. I asked the little girl where her "mamma" was and she told me she wasn't home but that her "nonna" was. That caught me off guard. I was under the impression the woman I was about to meet was much younger than I would expect a grandmother to be. I heard a toilet flush down the hall and then Carmela, who had just celebrated her thirtieth birthday on her day of release, walked into the room. "Nonna," the little girl said. "The signora is here."

Carmela sat on a cushion in what was clearly her usual chair at the small wooden kitchen table. Her narrow shoulders looked like a wire hanger and her sharp collarbones protruded from under a silky red blouse with a pattern of tiny triangles woven into the material. She wore rings on all her fingers, including her thumbs, that seemed to possess varying degrees of value, from cheap costume jewelry to ten-carat gold.

We sat at the table and I asked her about the decor. She said she loved the country kitchen look after seeing it in a documentary about the American Midwest and that she really wanted to visit Wyoming, which she pronounced as Yie-yo-ming, one day. I didn't correct her. As we spoke, a man came out of the back bedroom wearing a tank top and gray dress pants. He did not greet me or Carmela or the little girl. He went over to a pair of faded red wingback chairs in the sitting room. They looked like they had been fished out of a dumpster. Over the back of one was draped a neatly folded button-down shirt. He put it on and walked out without saying anything.

Carmela and I continued talking as if nothing had happened.

"How is reintegration into society?" I asked rather naively. She had not testified against anyone and had served her sentence completely, so she had no reason to worry about a vendetta or anything else, but I sensed that rehabilitation was not a goal or, more likely, an option. She explained that a lot had happened while she was inside and that she had a lot of catching up to do. Many old phone numbers now don't work, and some people she knew had died one way or another.

Part of our agreement was that Carmela was never supposed to be the primary subject of interest in my writing. Before she had gone to prison she had once worked for a local journalist, she explained. She told me she knew what reporters were looking for. I understood that what she really wanted was to not give too much of her own story away or inadvertently incriminate herself while still making some extra cash. She served us espresso in white plastic cups while we waited for her mother to arrive to babysit the little girl.

Carmela's mother let herself in about a half hour later. She couldn't have been more than fifty years old. I said hello and she politely nodded my way without saying a word, clearly understanding that I was a foreigner and in a way all foreigners, no matter how fluent we are in the language, feel suddenly mute when someone squints our way as if they cannot understand a single thing we say.

She scurried to the back of the apartment with the little girl. I had not had a chance to see if there was a structure built onto the end of the shipping crate, but from the inside this curious rooftop home seemed much larger than it had looked from the outside. Months later when I went back to the building to look around, I realized that the shipping container was actually balanced between two different buildings like a makeshift bridge. I struggled to remember what the flooring of the container was like because from the street level the bottom looked very worn out, as if it might give way at any time.

With her mother out of the room, Carmela put the envelope with my money in the back of the freezer. We left the country-kitchen shipping container and took the elevator down to the ground floor. I wondered if the reason she had told me to walk up the steps and not take the lift was to make sure everyone in the building got a look at who was coming in alone and that no one recognized me as a police officer, which implies a certain complicity—or accountability—among all the tenants. I wondered who lived in those other apartments, and if she had told them she had a visitor. Did she think a stranger might be tied to police or in some way threatening? I wondered as well if she could use the time it would take me to climb the stairs to hide something or someone, or to prepare for me. Or perhaps Carmela didn't want anyone to see her leave with me. I didn't ask, even though I was immensely curious.

Once out of the building, I followed her through the maze of hilly, cobbled streets in the Spanish Quarter. Overhead, laundry, flags, soccer banners, and advertisements for pizza joints flapped in the sea breeze that sweeps through Naples most hours of the day.

We headed toward the base of a long stairway that leads up to the Vomero hill, where affluent Neapolitans look down over the mess of the city below and out to sweeping views of Vesuvius, Capri, and beyond. On the way there, we circled around one block at least twice, which I assumed was either to make sure I could never find Carmela's apartment on my own or to lose someone who was trailing us.

We arrived in front of a narrow postwar high-rise. Carmela buzzed one of the plastic name buttons on the central intercom twice and then pushed through the building's unlocked main door. We walked up two flights of stairs and a pretty woman who looked a lot like a young Sophia Loren opened the door before we could knock. She was wearing a tight, shiny electric-blue wraparound shirt and faded jeans. Her extremely long fingernails were done up in a French manicure, and she smelled like the same Chanel perfume I wear.

I agreed not to publish any of the real names of any of the Camorra ex-cons, so we will call this woman Sophia. She grew up in Pupetta's hometown Castellammare di Stabia and said she "had a lot of respect for what she did to set the murder of her husband right." Sophia's dark eyes welled with tears when she explained how she, too, was pregnant when she went into prison but had a miscarriage early on. "They gave me poison and it killed my baby," she told me without a hint of doubt. "They did that to other girls, too."

Sophia opened a pack of Diana cigarettes and smoked one

after another as she explained that her father was killed in a mafia hit when she was still an infant and that her mother re-married a couple of times, before she died of breast cancer when Sophia was twelve.

"I've been on my own since then," she says. "I've never even had a serious boyfriend." The father of her miscarried baby apparently didn't count. From time to time Carmela asked me in the same Neapolitan dialect Sophia spoke if I was following what she was saying. I answered yes, but made notes to go over with Carmela to clarify anything I didn't quite follow.

Sophia's story is tragic but not altogether rare for this part of Italy. Girls without a proper crime family to back them will never be given a true opportunity to climb any mafia organization's hierarchy and will forever be condemned to the dregs of the group, either as drug runners or petty criminals. And without a powerful name, she is not even marriage material because she brings no promise of alliance to the table. "I started running drugs for my friend's dad," she says when I ask her to tell me about what led her to prison. "When the police were onto us, I was the obvious one to take the fall since there was no one protecting me."

Her time in jail was extremely difficult, she said. No one sent her money or brought her food or clothing, so she ended up "working" for some of the other women to make some cash for tobacco to roll her own cigarettes. "It was tough," she says, looking down at the table. "You really are alone in moments like that."

When I asked her what sort of "work" she could do in prison for the other women, she looked at Carmela nervously. She then explained that she had to be like a maid, washing the other women's clothes and doing whatever they wanted. I tried to press her about rumors I'd heard of prostitution rings inside female prisons, but she wouldn't bite.

The longer we talked, the more nervous Sophia became. She started looking at her text messages and checking the time every two or three minutes. Finally, she gave Carmela a look that prompted Carmela to tell me that it was time for us to go. I understood immediately that if we didn't, it could be bad for Sophia, or maybe even all of us. When we opened the door to leave, I was shocked to see a man standing in the hallway just a few steps from the door. He clearly knew Carmela. He grabbed her arm very tightly and said something to her in Neapolitan dialect that was incomprehensible to me. He looked through me as if I weren't there at all.

Carmela and I walked down the stairs without saying a word until we got out of the building. I was truly terrified but tried not to show it. I asked if we got Sophia into trouble and she told me that Sophia could handle herself. I asked her if the man was a trick or a pimp or maybe even a drug dealer or client—he fit the physical description of any of those in my mind. Carmela just looked at me like I was a child asking if Santa Claus was real.

"Who knows?" she said, even though I knew she certainly did.

We walked out of the Spanish Quarter and past the ancient San Carlo opera house and into the tony area along the Riviera di Chiaia, which offers some of the most amazing views of the good side of Vesuvius to be had anywhere in the city. It is the postcard vantage point—the exact opposite side of the volcano you see from Castellammare di Stabia. There we met a woman I'll call Rita, who Carmela explained had been arrested as an accessory to murder after getting caught with her then-boyfriend, a Camorra hit man. Rita said she had no idea her lover was out on a hit when he asked her to drive his car alongside a truck on a back road. "He just pulled the gun out of nowhere and started shooting," Rita said. "I was shocked."

I asked her why she didn't testify against him to save herself from jail, knowing full well she was lying to me. I had read the criminal dossier from her arrest and her fingerprints were on one of the weapons that she had helped reload.

"They would have killed me if I did that," she says. Her erstwhile boyfriend is still in prison but she has no intention of getting together when he gets out. "We had only just met," she explained. "Anyway, he was married."

Rita now works at her aunt's fur storage and seamstress shop, which cold-stores wealthy Neapolitans' fox and mink stoles for the winter. Rita does finish work on hems and replaces torn-off buttons on the furs and designer clothes. "Our clients are quite wealthy," she explained in a way I understood to mean they had benefited from various criminal enterprises. Later, I looked up the fur shop, which was registered as a dry cleaner under a man's name.

Rita's parents were both killed in a drive-by shooting when she was in her teens and she has lived with her aunt her whole life—which is divided into periods before and after prison. Her uncle died by suicide a few years ago.

"Pills," she said, when I asked how he took his life. A classic mafia suicide method is a cyanide pill to avoid being arrested, but I thought it better not to ask what kind of drug he'd taken. It seemed redundant to confirm what was implied.

Rita explained that she had a series of Camorra boyfriends who "were always sweet" but never wanted to settle down. The reality was that because she, like Sophia, didn't come from a strong mafia family, she was a convenient mistress but not exactly marriage material.

Four days after our interview, Rita was arrested for drug trafficking out of her aunt's shop in a sting operation that netted more than a dozen Camorristi. Two months later, Sophia was back in prison for drug peddling, too. There is no real chance of rehabilitation for so many women caught up in crime. Even if they wanted to get out of a criminal organization, they would have to turn state's evidence to leave. And for many, the risk that such good behavior carries is far too great. Carmela disappeared after our day together, too. Or at least she never answered my messages or phone calls again.

The first time I met Pietro, the ex-con and advocate for tortured inmates, I asked him if he was afraid or felt like he was in danger for helping women when they got out of tough prisons. Naturally, I assumed his group was trying to rehabilitate the ex-prisoners so they could start a clean life. "Why would I be afraid?" he said. "Everyone is very grateful I'm there to help their sons and daughters and friends get back on their feet."

Some argue that the main reason there are so many more women associated with organized crime today is that only now do police recognize and arrest them. Others argue[1] that as organized-crime syndicates have evolved, they have moved away from sheer violence and added more white-collar crimes to their portfolios, which has driven a need for a more educated criminal. Women in southern Italy tend to stay in school longer, and in cases of mafia families, some of the females are sent to be educated abroad. While abroad, they have ended up casing out the local culture to see if there was a weak spot for infiltration, all while appearing to be removed from their criminal families back home.

Whatever is driving up the numbers, at the time of publication, the Italian Ministry of Justice confirms there are more than 150 women in Italy's prisons serving time for mafia crimes—the highest number ever recorded.

Joining an organized-crime group is not like signing up for a club you can try out and eventually leave if you don't like it or if membership isn't quite what you had expected. Nor can you just choose to join. If someone is not born into a crime family, they must be chosen and recommended, which is mirrored in other aspects of Italian society in which the best jobs are given to those with a raccomandata, or weighty recommendation. Interested men who do not come from a criminal family are sponsored, and if they mess up, the sponsor is without exception killed first. Most sons and daughters of mafiosi don't actively decide whether continuing the criminal life is for them. The only choice to be made is if one day they want to leave, and that's generally only by death or with the help of police.

Though by now a household name, the 'Ndrangheta syndicate is a relative newcomer on the global organized-crime scene, transitioning from a largely rural mafia that made money on extortion, kidnapping, and small-scale smuggling in the 1990s when it entered the international drug-smuggling market.

The group calls its clusters *'ndrine* (singular *'ndrina*) and not "clans," as the Neapolitan Camorra refers to its groups. Its horizontal power structure is similar to that of the Neapolitan group, with lots of bosses of groups of families holding the same level of power instead of everyone under one big don. Family bloodlines are key, and traditionally we have been told that women are largely kept out of the most important decisions, though there are several notable exceptions that point to a more important role than perhaps experts have been willing to admit, especially in the context of southern Italy where misogyny is rampant. Alessandra Cerreti says that the role of women within the criminal groups is as different as the groups themselves. In the Camorra, which she says is far more liberal, there are even lesbian bosses. In the 'Ndrangheta, women are instead mostly charged with indoctrinating the children to keep the force of evil alive.

Italy has often been called a country that feminism forgot, and it is apparent in nearly every sector of life. I spent a great deal of time with Laura Boldrini when she spoke at a Women in the World event in New York City on the heels of the #MeToo movement. She was there as one of the most vocal female Italian politicians, having served as speaker of the lower house of parliament, to date the highest-ranking role a woman has ever held on Italy's political spectrum. But what she was there to discuss was the horrific abuse she had faced for speaking out about how women are treated. She was receiving death and rape threats on social media that she then re-upped to expose the senders. But instead of acting as a deterrent, revealing the abuse just made it worse. Even the then interior minister

Matteo Salvini of the far-right Lega party got into the act, taking a blow-up sex doll on stage during a rally and saying it looked like Boldrini's twin.

Fewer than half of Italian women work outside the home, and when they do they are met with job titles and descriptions that show a preference for males—there are no feminine versions of the words minister or lawyer, for example, which Boldrini says is because women were excluded from the job market for so long. "Feminism is a dirty word in Italy," she says. "People are afraid to use it, as if it is somehow threatening to be seen as a feminist."

In the southern regions of Italy, this is especially true, and women are often stifled both inside the home and in the workplace. The 'Ndrangheta family dynamics are complicated to parse, but it is clear that as the crime group has established itself as an international criminal entity, women are an integral part of the puzzle.

The 'Ndrangheta's first real headlines outside of Italy came when they were ultimately held responsible for the 1973 kidnapping of American oil baron John Paul Getty's grandson for a ransom of $17 million, which they had hoped would be easier to get than it was. The elder Getty assumed his wayward grandson, who had decamped in Rome with his mother, was trying to swindle money out of him, never believing that the 'Ndrangheta existed or, if they did, that they actually had him until they sent the boy's mother the top of his ear. Eventually, Getty talked the mobsters down to a sum of around $2 million and the boy was released.

The scenes depicted in a 2017 film about the case, *All the*

Money in the World, do little justice to the depths of brutality most of the 'Ndrangheta's kidnapping victims suffer as the gang tries to bargain for their ransom. Many kidnapping victims whose families couldn't pay, or refused to pay, were literally picked apart as punishment or dissolved in acid limb by limb until they died. Although Getty losing his ear is a true story, it is tame compared to what really goes on. John Paul Getty's grandson either suffered more than he ever admitted or the group went easy on him, perhaps because a behind-the-scenes deal had been made.

Daughters in the 'Ndrangheta are often forced into arranged marriages between like-minded family 'ndrine, sometimes put forward by fathers as a peace or truce offering to settle a feud.[2] This keeps the women in what may appear to be subservient roles. While many mafia historians have not seen advancements for women in the 'Ndrangheta as often as in other criminal groups in the country, women do play a key role in keeping up the criminal cycle.

The prosecutor Cerreti is one of the first people to take women's roles in the 'Ndrangheta seriously. She is a petite brunette with piercing eyes and a sharp sense of character. She can read most people she encounters in her line of work before even opening their criminal dossier.

The door to her office in the tribunal of Reggio Calabria was a bulletproof mass of solid metal, reinforced to withstand a car bomb if someone had managed to breach the fortified courthouse's external protective barrier, a genuine fear when she became the rising star of Italy's anti-mafia army there in 2013. She had just convinced 'Ndrangheta daughter Giuseppina "Giusy"

Pesce to turn against her family, which led to the arrest and sentencing of around eighty clan thugs, including Pesce's own father. In the courtroom, Salvatore Pesce threatened to kill Cerreti and her husband, who is conveniently an anti-mafia Carabinieri officer, which amounted to ordering a hit on the prosecutor's life. Pesce did not threaten publicly to kill his own daughter, but it was understood that Giuseppina's life was in danger, too.

The attention launched Cerreti to become one of the most powerful female anti-mafia prosecutors in Italy. She had cut her teeth investigating terror insurgents in Milan in 2005, just two years after the CIA and Italian secret service had snatched Egyptian cleric Abu Omar off the streets of Milan to allegedly torture him as part of the Bush administration's "global war on terrorism." She then moved south to take on one of the deadliest criminal syndicates anywhere in the world.

I met Cerreti in early 2021 in Milan, where she was flanked by two bodyguards. But rather than a bulletproof door, she sat behind plexiglass in her upper floor office in the Milan tribunal. Her hair had grown longer since she worked in Calabria and she wore a pink FFP2 mask. She is again focused on pulling up the deep roots of the 'Ndrangheta and Sicilian Cosa Nostra here in the wealthier north, working to chip away at the far reaches of the groups. She has been under constant police protection since Pesce's threat.

She believes very much that women play a vital role in all of Italy's organized crime syndicates, and knows they are the key to keeping crime families together. As such, they are also instrumental in tearing them apart, especially if Cerreti can convince them to give evidence for the sake of their children.

"A mother who acts in the interests of her children is impossible to stop," she told me, underscoring that women who testified could tear the group apart at its seams, making female turncoats especially dangerous to crime groups.

Cerreti doesn't look the part of the important role she plays as a strong arm in Italian justice. She is confident in the way many lawyers are, but her sense of irony and humor offer a more unguarded side than one might expect. I liked her immediately, despite the fact that she is flanked by plainclothes bodyguards with pistols strapped to their chests. She laughs easily, despite what is undoubtedly an unthinkable responsibility. Every woman she convinces to turn against the criminal family runs a risk of being murdered. There is little in the way of forgiveness for being truthful, and Cerreti is well aware of the weight of these important witnesses. But don't call them pentiti, she said. "They are never penitent." She prefers the term *collaboratore di giustizia*, "collaborator of justice." Without exception, she says, in a statement that contradicts the machoism synonymous with mafia culture, men always collaborate to save themselves while women collaborate to save their children.

Her goal was to end what she has called a "predestination" within the criminal group that trains young boys to handle knives and firearms as preteens and young girls to accept that they will eventually be offered as nothing short of currency, traded for vendettas or married off to create alliances. "Children are the key," she said. "But it isn't without its challenges."

She believes that women will continue to be considered vital components of the criminal groups in the court of law. For instance, a Milan court in 2000 was the first to convict a woman as a "sister in omertà," finding her to be a "full-fledged 'Ndrangheta member,"[3] though even turncoats who knew her said it just wasn't true. She had power but was never officially inducted.

That's one of the ways women escaped judicial attention for so long. Those who study mafia groups have become somewhat blinded by the idea that only those who take part in the ritual are functioning members. The three Camorra women I met were clearly part of the organization, but by not being "initiated" into it; does that make them any less criminal?

That attitude of female subservience repeats itself in all layers of Italian society, both personal and professional. In my first years in Rome, I was shocked by the blatant misogyny that came in such subtle ways as asking me constantly to "send your husband," or even once when I was younger to "send your father" to discuss problems seen as male, including buying something at a hardware shop or dealing with mechanical issues with my car.

That attitude toward women is hard to come to terms with, but early on in my time in Italy, an Italian friend explained to me that it was easier to accept it and just use their lack of respect to fly under the radar. She advised me that fighting it would be exhausting and futile, but that most Italian women have learned how to exploit it. I remember interviewing a prominent Italian politician when I was heavily pregnant with my first son during a scorching summer day. All he kept saying was that I should not be working this late into the pregnancy, asking his assistant to bring me water. He insisted I should have my feet elevated and that I needed a cushion to sit on, at times even criticizing my "American hard-nosed bosses" who would send a pregnant woman out on such a hot day. All the while I asked him questions that ended in a story full of revelations he would have surely never given me under any other circumstance.

Italians often look at American women differently than they do their own female demographic, in part because they know—or assume—that "we" won't put up with the usual crap Italian women tolerate. When the #MeToo movement first broke the sexual-hierarchy barrier, Italians were quick to dismiss the scandal in no small part because of the role Filipina-Italian model Ambra Battilana Gutierrez played by wearing a wire to catch Harvey Weinstein, an encounter many will remember only because he jacked off in a potted plant in front of her. Italians automatically felt that the fact that Ambra had been involved somehow lessened the crime. Italian newspapers predictably responded by running story after story alongside her sultry modeling shots, as if to say that any sexual abuse against her was certainly invited, and that recording the now-disgraced Hollywood mogul couldn't possibly have been her own clever idea.

Italy was one of the few Western countries that did not engage in a reckoning on its own sexual bias, and it is in no small part because women allow themselves to be written off, finding it easier, as my friend advised, not to rock the boat but to just work around it. Even my female Italian friends rolled their eyes at the #MeToo movement, finding it hard to believe that a woman could be forced to sleep with a boss or someone who held power over her. Not that they didn't do it in Italy, but it was just seen as a way to exploit male stupidity.

This is true in organized crime, where, time and again,

women are committing heinous crimes in the group's name without police noticing. Even when these women earn the dubious respect that goes with their criminal success, they are discounted by law enforcement because "women don't belong to the mafia." Nonetheless, the increasing number of criminal investigations into women and horrific violence at their hands makes it hard to believe that just because they cannot be sworn into the boys' club, their actions—whether murder or money laundering—don't count. Perhaps they, too, are just playing along and using the blatant misogyny to fly under the radar.

Cerreti told me that mafia women's primary task is to help teach the children wrong from right. Where most parents might teach a child to forgive and forget, the 'Ndrangheta mother teaches that revenge is, in fact, not only acceptable but expected. She must ingrain in her offspring the clear-cut gender roles and responsibilities to help pass down the criminal culture, and also dissuade in her children any rebellion that could lead to respect for the law and the potential betrayal of the clan.

With few exceptions, mafia women are born into or marry into crime families and can only leave in a coffin or by testifying against their parents, siblings, or husbands. They invariably normalize criminality, making excuses for heinous crimes and rationalizing everything from extortion to murder. As mothers, their chief role is to indoctrinate their children into the life of crime, essentially teaching them bad from good and that vendetta is preferable to forgiveness.

Later, when their children are grown, mafia mammas will offer them iron-clad alibis, hide their contraband under their beds, defend them publicly, and take their abuse.

Those maternal roles are clear, but it is increasingly evident that women are more than mothers in these syndicates. If prisons can be crime schools that develop hardened criminals, then the mafia family home is the kindergarten where the groundwork is carefully laid to enculturate tomorrow's men of honor. A forty-six-year-old 'Ndrangheta dad named Agostino Cambareri was arrested in 2019 for making his eight-year-old son cut cocaine and bag up marijuana for sale. Police say the boy also reportedly helped spread dirt on at least one shallow grave of a man his father had killed. There was reportedly no coffin involved in the burial, according to a turncoat who was there. If Cambareri had not been arrested, it could have been another ten years of learning at his father's knee before the child was old enough to be truly initiated.

Consider, too, 'Ndrangheta daughter Rita Di Giovine (whose disastrous family history we will get to later), who was forced from an early age to stuff precise heroin doses into shampoo bottles for her criminal mother. Rita, one of the most important and penitent witnesses in the 'Ndrangheta, was arrested while holding a thousand ecstasy tablets she was being forced to smuggle. Her mafia mom couldn't be initiated, but does that make her any less a criminal than Agostino Cambareri?

Pupetta's first son, Pasqualino, disappeared without a trace after he was supposed to meet his mother's new lover, Umberto Ammaturo. The man had promised to indoctrinate Pasqualino into the Camorra. Pupetta, for all her documented faults, would have done anything for the boy—and for all her children— except collaborate with law enforcement to get justice for her son.

She would not speak to me about Pasqualino's fate. Each time we met I asked and each time she stopped the conversation with a look of angst that didn't quite reach remorse but could have been regret of some sort. "It's too painful to remember that period," she said. But in the mid-1990s, she did tell journalist Clare Longrigg[4] that she was sure Ammaturo, with whom she had twins, was ultimately responsible for her first son's death, and that the only thing she wanted to know for sure was where her then lover had buried him. It seems impossible to imagine the level of brainwashing it would take to remain silent for decades about the fact that the father of your younger children likely killed your eldest. And did so why? Because the boy was the son of a rival clan member who had been dead for more than two decades.

Time and again, women like Cerreti—who butt their heads against a loyalty stronger than common sense—try to chip away at the tradition of protecting evil. Any gains she makes can come at a terrible cost for the women who betray their criminal families, but if this toxic bond can be broken, she knows the fissure can lead to arrests and convictions and ultimately save lives.

3

The Strong and the Sweet

"I dissociated myself in order to start my life again. I do not think with hindsight; it is useless to wonder if today I would do things differently."

While Pupetta sat in prison for killing her first husband's assassin, her guards had to play traffic cop to the many suitors who clamored to visit her. Love songs and poetry were written about this brave and beautiful murderess, and she reveled in the attention she says helped her bide the time.

Pupetta shuddered when I asked her about raising a baby in Naples' notorious Poggioreale prison. She was allowed to keep him in her dark corner cell until he turned four. I told her about my own children, both sons, and she asked to see photos of them. As I scrolled through some old ones I kept on my phone, she seemed grandmotherly. I explained to her that my children were raised in Italy while their grandparents lived in the United States and Canada, and that they had just a passing relationship with them, which had always made me sad. She then told me about her own grandmother's disappointment that she had married Pasqualone, how her grandmother had hoped that Pupetta might meet someone outside the usual crowd, which I took to mean the criminal underworld.

"I disappointed her," Pupetta said. "I have never been judgmental about what my own children choose to do because I was so hurt that she didn't respect my choices."

After I left her house, I looked up her family history to learn that both of her grandmothers had died in the 1940s, long before Pupetta would have ever met Pasqualone. What was the purpose of the lie, I wondered. Was it to get me to trust her, or had she confused the grandmother with an aunt or other female relative she held in high esteem? At the time I thought that maybe she just wanted to be relatable, but surely she knew I would check her every story. When I went back for what at the time I did not know would be our final visit before her daughter, Antonella, told me never to come back, I asked Pupetta whether the grandmother who had disliked Pasqualone was maternal or paternal—I hadn't asked at the time. She looked at me and smiled and quickly dismissed the subject.

Raising a child in a prison as hard as Poggioreale gave Pupetta certain perks other inmates didn't have, even though the circumstances made the experience anything but joyful. Unlike the general female population, who lived in large dormitory-style rooms with triple bunk beds and a single toilet in the corner, incarcerated mothers were given single- or double-occupancy cells with wooden boxes on the floor beside their beds, inlaid with tiny mattresses for their babies. Pasqualino had a small selection of toys and a few books, and she got to take him out to play in the prison playground once or twice a day. But Pupetta mostly made up games to play or sang to him as they sat together on the cold cement floor of her cell.

Pasqualino's first friends were the children of other incarcerated mafia women, many of whom were serving short sentences as accomplices or accessories to crimes committed by their men. After they got out, they didn't forget the godmother in the corner cell. Pupetta laughed as she recounted some of the things her former inmate girlfriends snuck into Poggioreale when they visited her, from local white wine to truffles. She was the rare female inmate locked up in the 1950s for murder. Her long sentence gave her seniority, and her crime garnered automatic respect from all the new inmates.

She had done a man's job by avenging her husband's death and there were no other women who could say the same. In a crime school like this, she was both valedictorian and class bully. The other inmates did her bidding, and even changed Pasqualino's soiled diapers during open recreation time or babysat when she needed a break from his crying. The stories of her incarceration that were published at the time vary in remarkable ways from her own memory, or the stories she chooses to tell. Undoubtedly it is one's right to recast their own story—even one that has been lived in crime dockets like Pupetta's—but the ease with which she chooses to rewrite hers entirely is sometimes mind-boggling.

What is known for sure is that during her incarceration, wedding proposals and gifts floated in from the outside almost daily, mostly from Camorristi who wanted to latch on to her rising star when she got out. But it was inside where she flexed her muscle as she ruled the top of the hierarchy among the imprisoned wives and girlfriends. She set up a system inside much like her late husband's on the outside, in which she doled out "favors" to inmates who could then source information from their own visitors about what was happening on the outside, which Pupetta would pass along to favorable clansmen of her choice.

On Pasqualino's fourth birthday, he was taken from Pupetta's jail cell to start school and live with her mother. By the time Pupetta got out of prison, when Pasqualino was ten, he was calling his grandmother "Mamma."

Freed, Pupetta was clearly ready to move on and start her new life, describing her release from prison as something of a rebirth. At the time she sought out the press, gave interviews to show that she was back, and courted various directors, trying to carve out a new career in film. "It was both terrifying and liberating," she explained to me. She gave a number of interviews in which she berated the prison system, its treatment of her and other inmates, even though she had earned a number of special privileges during her final years inside. After so many years away at "crime school," rehabilitation was not to be part of that new beginning, even though she says she had fully intended to live a cleaner life when she got out of prison. She felt no remorse whatsoever for the murder she'd committed, in fact she has always said she would do it again, even now in her eighties. She felt that it was her duty, which was a mix of her father's principles and her newlywed husband's influence over her. Had she not killed Big Tony, she would have likely been shuffled off to marry an associate, forgotten forever, reduced to being just another Camorristi wife. Pupetta wanted a different legacy. She did not need to avenge her husband's death. Society did not demand it of her, especially in the 1950s. Without the influence of social media and the Internet, she acted in a vacuum and could have easily gotten away, quite literally, with murder.

There was a sense in the way she presented herself both in person and in recent media interviews that she had even fewer regrets in old age, that somehow her life had been well lived. There is no question that she enjoyed her notorious legacy, and I am completely convinced she would have reveled in the fact that the police in Naples prohibited a public funeral for her when she died. When I went to her gravesite to lay flowers, I was told I could not, that her life could not be celebrated, that too many "mafiosi" are sent off gloriously. I know she would have loved to be considered too important to be celebrated publicly. I left the flowers on a nearby grave.

One can only imagine a figure like Pupetta in the age of Instagram. She was able to create an alluring image of a woman in complete control, with her leather dresses, choke collars, and lowcut blouses, without a single follower or like. She often said to me, "Tell the Americans this," when she told me a story. I often thought she would love the idea that people outside Italy would read about her.

She could summon the press, attract multiple men, and make decisions people listened to, despite the fact that she was a woman who nobody believed could actually be part of the mafia. As prosecutor Cerreti saw it, though, Pupetta was an early influencer of her own. She knew well that the image of the brazen "mafia woman" would carry some clout in the outside world, even if she possessed little in the way of organizational authority to back it up. "She is a self-made woman in many ways, both when she committed murder and how she chooses to portray herself today," Cerreti told me.

A few years after Pupetta's release in 1965, one of the women she had befriended in prison set her up on a blind date with Umberto Ammaturo, a square-jawed Camorra underboss with dark wavy hair. He groomed his thick sideburns to perfection with a straight razor he is rumored to have used to carve up more than one enemy. He was not her beloved Pasqualone, but he was sexy, and after all that time in prison Pupetta was lonely. More important, he was a Camorra underboss—meaning that settling on him would not result in her stepping backward from Pasqualone's standing. That said, she might have taken Ammaturo's nickname, 'o pazzo, "the crazy one," as a warning of what was to come.

As handler of the Camorra's emerging cocaine routes in and out of South America, Umberto was fluent in Spanish. He was also hotheaded. He had a short temper that Pupetta said often turned to violent outbursts against her and Pasqualino, who had moved back in with her when she left prison.

Umberto had started his criminal career as a guaglione, essentially a street kid who pickpocketed tourists and stood as a lookout for cops in order to warn the bigger criminals. He caught the eye of more seasoned men, who admired his deviance. He quickly climbed the criminal ladder, advancing to a full-time cigarette smuggler for the Camorra in the early 1960s.

He had connections to Tommaso Buscetta,[1] one of the Sicilian Mafia's most notable turncoats, who is personally responsible for the dismantling of the Cosa Nostra in the 1990s by
testifying in Italy's so-called Maxi Trials. After Buscetta died of
cancer, it was revealed that he and his family had gone to live
in Florida under new identities with full police protection for
many years. Buscetta had testified against some of the biggest
mobsters in Sicily and the United States in epic hearings that
ran from February 10, 1986, to January 30, 1992.

Those trials led to a number of American mafia arrests and
launched the career of one young district attorney in New York
named Rudolph Giuliani. Thanks to Buscetta and another
turncoat's testimony, 338 people were convicted and sentenced
to a total of 2,665 years in prison. (Giuliani went on to become
one of the most successful anti-mafia prosecutors in US history
and brought hundreds of criminals to justice.)

Umberto and Pupetta hit it off immediately. A few months
after they started a relationship, Pupetta, at the age of thirty-
one, was pregnant with twins. Not long after Antonella and
Roberto were born, Umberto was arrested in Naples with the
Camorra's top man, who lorded over the various emerging
criminal enterprises in northern Italy. The two were charged
with smuggling cocaine from Latin America via the diplomatic
mail pouch of Panama's consulate in Milan. During the ensuing trial, Umberto faked a number of health conditions, including insanity, with the help of the Camorra-friendly forensic
psychiatrist Aldo Semerari. Thanks to the crooked doc, Umberto ultimately escaped hard jail time and was sentenced to an
psychiatric hospital—from which he quickly escaped.

Pupetta and Umberto never married, but they worked hard to elevate their joint criminal interests during their first years together. In November 1967, Pupetta was convicted of receiving stolen goods when a hundred shirts mysteriously arrived at the clothing shop she had recently opened in Naples without an invoice or purchase order, either of which would have required her to pay tax. She was acquitted of delinquent activity and never served her three-month sentence. She was investigated numerous times throughout the late 1960s and early 1970s and frequently found herself on the periphery of a variety of crimes.

When Pasqualino reached his teens, there was tension in the house. Pupetta's firstborn was handsome and built like his robust dad, and Pupetta often reminisced about her dead husband when her son turned a certain way or smiled just so. Pasqualino started to rebel and compete with Umberto, who didn't like the constant reminder of Pupetta's previous life. Pasqualino's temperament didn't help, and he often lashed out about how his mother's lover would never be a replacement for his own dead father—a man Pasqualino had never met.

When he started mouthing off to Umberto and eventually threatened to avenge the death of his father—a job his mother had taken care of just fine—the tension in the household reached a boiling point.

In 1972, a few days after Pasqualino's eighteenth birthday, Umberto set up an appointment with him under the guise of a truce, offering to help the budding criminal develop some of his own contacts within the construction arm of the Camorra. The two made plans to meet at a dusty Neapolitan construction site where a new tangenziale, toll bypass, was being built. The superhighway would allow travelers to skirt the stifling Neapolitan gridlock to reach the Amalfi Coast and deep southern provinces more quickly. It would also line the pockets of dozens of Camorra clans that had infiltrated nearly every aspect of the project.

The meeting happened to be on the day that crews were pouring the cement foundation for the supporting pillars of the massive four-lane highway. There were more than a dozen mixer trucks working furiously to set the steel framework into deep pockets that had been dug into the lower foothills of Mount Vesuvius. The hot wind blew thick clouds of dust through the site as the noisy trucks rolled in and out.

Pasqualino was never seen again after that day, in a vanishing act that had all the markings of what the Camorra calls a lupara bianca—an assassination carried out with such precision that there is no trace of the body left at all.

As is so often the case in crime families, life becomes a sort of currency that can be easily spent or saved depending on a variety of circumstances. Pupetta would not talk to me about the disappearance and presumed murder of her son by her lover, brushing off each question with the flick of her black-manicured hand, assuring me that I can look it up. "I've talked about it too much already," she said.

Without a confession—which, until her death, she still hoped would one day come from a turncoat—she had no choice but to assume her son's grave is under the base of the tangenziale pillar. She would not confirm to me whether she was responsible for the flowers that appeared there every year on Pasqualino's birthday—until the area became a rogue dumping ground for the mob's toxic garbage enterprise.

Despite the assumptions Pupetta harbored, she and Umberto still went on to forge a criminal coupledom that eventually landed them a joint conviction for the murder and decapitation of Aldo Semerari, the shady shrink who helped spring Umberto from prison by signing off on his phony mental illness years earlier.

Semerari disappeared under suspicious circumstances from the Royal Hotel in Naples in late March 1982. His body, from the neck down, was found a week later in the trunk of a burned-out car with his decapitated head on the front seat. He had been tortured, based on the broken bones and cuts, and hung upside down to bleed out, undoubtedly while he was still alive—an extra cruel touch that was meant as a warning for others. When I asked a forensic scientist how difficult it would have been for Pupetta and Umberto, working separately or together, to behead the doctor, I was told they would likely have needed to use an electric saw, which cuts through bone much more easily than a blade. The fact that Semerari had no blood left in his body would also have made it an easier—and cleaner—job.

A day later, Semerari's personal assistant, Fiorella Carrara, was found dead in her home with a Magnum .357 sticking out of her mouth. Her death was classified as a suicide, even though her fingerprints were not on the gun and she left no note, and three days after her body was discovered her home was ransacked and storage boxes were mysteriously removed from her attic. The investigation into Semerari's decapitation initially focused on his political ties, but quickly turned to Pupetta and Umberto as primary suspects.

Semerari had ties to Italy's far-right movement, which was involved in a string of nationwide terrorist attacks during a two-decade period referred to as the Years of Lead, so called for the sheer number of bullets used in terrorist attacks during the late 1960s to the 1980s. At the time, extreme right-wing and left-wing organizations were waging a war on the establishment—and on each other. The unrest wasn't mafia related, but there were a number of people like Semerari who had their fingers in both pools of blood. Semerari was also a member of the Propaganda Due Masonic lodge, which included several of Italy's most prestigious secret service members. It included a few hold-out Americans who were stationed in Italy after the war to keep communism at bay, and also had charter lodges in Brazil and Argentina. The lodge counted up-and-coming politician Silvio Berlusconi, who would later become one of Italy's longest-serving prime ministers, on its roster. The Freemasons—much like the mafia and even the Catholic Church—didn't allow women to be members, but many were loosely associated, albeit on the periphery. The many alliances forged by the lodge likely kept Semerari out of jail, and many initially assumed they led to his death.

Pupetta adamantly denies any role in murdering and decapitating Semerari, though she did describe Carrara to me as a putana, "whore." She described Semerari as a traitor for helping their rival Raffaele Cutolo, underscoring the extent to which she and Umberto had a motive to kill him. Betrayal in crime circles is without question the greatest unforgiveable sin, and even though Umberto eventually betrayed Pupetta and the larger circle, he, too, found Semerari's betrayal in helping Cutolo a step too far.

Cutolo, nicknamed the Professor for his elegant demeanor, had threatened Pupetta and Umberto's criminal livelihood when he launched the Nuova Camorra Organizzata, or New Camorra Organization, known as the NCO, on October 24, 1970. She spoke of him with the type of hatred one might associate with an unfaithful ex-husband. Her eyes narrowed and her mouth pursed as she said his name.

Cutolo's new group was a conglomerate of clans that was perfectly positioned to wipe out Pupetta and Umberto's various enterprises when he launched it, a sort of direct hit from within on their criminal success, which allegedly included managing extortion rings, collecting the pizzo, or protection money, and money laundering. The fact that the group had sprung from within the Camorra itself made the couple's sense of betrayal far worse than a push into their business by the rival Cosa Nostra or even 'Ndrangheta. The Camorra clans were notorious for their infighting, but Cutolo's threat to the cohesion of the crime group was worse because he threatened to take his clans to form another group. Cutolo fancied himself something of a cross between Jesus Christ and the magician David Copperfield, insisting that he could both forgive sins and read minds, which somehow enticed clansmen to follow him. (When Semerari's burned-out Fiat was found, it was parked in front of the house of Cutolo's driver—no doubt left as a message for anyone else thinking of switching alliances.)

Semerari, a balding stick figure of a man, betrayed Pupetta

and Umberto by writing a series of fake diagnoses that allowed Cutolo to escape a prison term, exactly as he once had done for Umberto. Had Cutolo been put away, his NCO would have more easily been kept from interfering with Pupetta and Umberto's trajectory, which he undermined by sending his own clans to do work they were doing. Instead, thanks to Semerari, Cutolo served his term in a minimum-security psychiatric hospital from where he could—and easily did—run most aspects of the new criminal enterprise.

Visitors could come and go as they pleased, and Cutolo could have also easily walked out, given that it was a minimum security setting and he had furlough rights, but he chose instead to escape by blasting through one of the asylum's unfortified brick walls a few months before his scheduled release date.

Cutolo's NCO was in a bitter and bloody civil war with another new conglomerate of clans that had popped up to hold his group at bay. The Nuova Famiglia, or New Family, known as NF, was made up of some of the Camorra's hardest fighters, and staunchly supported by a dear friend of Pupetta's named Carmine Alfieri. Though he looked like a strict high school principal, Alfieri supported the old-style Camorra lawlessness—the physical threats and vendettas that neither Pupetta nor Umberto wanted to see replaced.

Nicknamed o 'Ntufato, "angry one," Alfieri supported the NF and helped it join forces with a faction in Sicily's Cosa Nostra, which gave it strategic regional power that included a large swath of southern Italy.[2] The NF was also supported by the Camorra's powerful Casalesi clan, the most well-known outside of Italy, and which is still considered the strongest of the Neapolitan clans.

Where Cutolo's NCO was able to "employ" disgruntled youth and stragglers and build up an army of thugs who could fight, the NF focused on loftier membership, like luring in politicians and police who could ultimately protect its members and insulate its criminal pursuits.

The strength of Cutolo's NCO came in part from another woman who flew under the radar because of her gender but who had outsized influence in the mafia, regardless. Cutolo's sister, Rosetta, secretly ran many of the meetings among clansmen while her brother was in prison. It is believed that he gave her general guidelines but trusted her enough to let her know how to conduct business on his behalf.

Rosetta, whose nickname was Occh'egghiaccio, "Ice Eyes," was clearly in control of her brother's affairs during his multiple incarcerations, which started in the 1960s and continue today. While in prison he has fathered two children, including one through artificial insemination with fresh sperm sneaked out by his wife during a visit. Pupetta despised Rosetta as well, describing her to me as a whore and insinuating that she slept with her brother, which in crime circles is punishable by death.

The fact was that Rosetta was her brother's most loyal supporter and his greatest critic, often chastising him for giving fiery speeches to journalists from his prison cell. Anti-mafia prosecutor Antonio Laudati was the first to prove that it was really Rosetta who was in charge. "Her brother has always been under the power of her forceful personality," he told Clare Longrigg. "He's been in prison for thirty years; during that time she became director of the Nuova Camorra Organizzata in her own right."

For the first fifteen years that she was running her incarcerated brother's business, she lived with her mother and took care of the family's substantial rose garden, all the while taking messages from her delinquent brother to various clan members she hosted in her mother's home. Her rise to power was in many ways aided by Pupetta, whose own trajectory, despite her being a woman, seemed unstoppable. Rosetta was the key negotiator with South American cocaine cartel leaders and the Sicilian Cosa Nostra—who, according to a turncoat who spoke to prosecutors, respected her cunning business acumen even as they refused to recognize her as anything but her brother's mouthpiece. But the truth of the matter was that she was making key decisions and informing him of them, not the other way around. She was brilliantly depicted as the mastermind she was in the 1986 film about the NCO, *Il Camorrista*—a role no one has ever publicly denied.

She was under constant surveillance by police, even though her brother insisted she was not involved at all in the clan's activities. The denial worked to some extent. But no amount of her brother's dismissal of her involvement, even as she fronted drug negotiations and peace talks with rival clans, could prevent her from eventually landing in trouble with the law. She lived as a fugitive after authorities tried her in absentia and sentenced her to nine years in prison for mafia-related crimes (though acquitted her on nine murder charges) in the late 1980s. She was arrested while hiding out in a convent in 1993 and served six years of her sentence. She told authorities at the time that she was tired of being a fugitive. She now lives in her hometown but refused to be interviewed.

In 2002, the academic Felia Allum interviewed Alfonso Ferrara Rosanova, the pentito son of an NCO clan boss, and the subject of Rosetta came up. He told her that Rosetta was fiercely protected by her brother, which he said "by no means excludes the determination and skills she deployed in achieving the NCO's goals."[3] He also told Allum that she was "no subordinate or passive bystander, but fully involved in the clan's activities and enabled it to survive while Raffaele was in prison."

Allum adds: "Rosetta demonstrates the limits of power conceded to Camorra women during this stage because the clan relied on her but did not want her to be seen as being involved or visibly active." In essence, Rosetta was the last of her kind of secret weapon before women became criminal protagonists in their own right.

The Cutolo siblings' NCO quickly dominated the Neapolitan crimescape, at one time supporting an estimated seven thousand members and their families.[4] Unlike other syndicates that have clear lines of power, Camorra bosses rule only those who will listen to them, with clans composed of group members who recognize a particular boss's leadership. It is the underbosses and smaller criminals who give power to the clan boss, but this dynamic also paves the way for lower-level criminals to change alliances and facilitates a lot of wasted time and loss of life as the lower-level criminals jockey for position.

The Camorra's looser structure also makes it easier for women to take a more central command because there is less of a line of succession, and harder to sidestep women with a high criminal acumen—especially if they are given a man's blessing to take the helm.

Allum says that after the era in which Rosetta Cutolo reigned in secret, the Camorra's structure eventually allowed women to become true protagonists "in their own right, either out of necessity or with criminal intent."

The Camorra's schizophrenic mentality and drifting allegiances eventually led to the demise of Cutolo's NCO, which fizzled out after most of its top leaders went to prison or were killed off in assassinations. The NF, supported by Pupetta and her allies, admitted to more than five hundred murders during its bloody war with the NCO between 1981 and 1983. But the victory was short-lived, and the NF also faded away after internal battles among member clans. The final insult arrived when Pupetta's dear friend Alfieri and other supporters eventually became pentiti.

Umberto and Pupetta were jointly convicted of Semerari's murder, but not before Umberto escaped—first to Africa and then Peru—leaving Pupetta on her own to face justice and raise their twins. Pupetta tried to run, too, but she was arrested as she left her home dressed like a Roma nomad—and with around $2 million in her handbag. Where the money came from is debatable, but the fact that she had it implies access to funds beyond her income, which at the time was officially negligible. She spent four more years in prison until both she and Umberto were acquitted on appeal in 1982, which led him to testify against his former clan. She grew bitter toward Umberto as the years passed and used her power to convince her twins, then just entering their teens, to turn their backs on their father, too.

The fact that Umberto left Pupetta alone to face criminal charges was not entirely uncommon among criminal couples.

Women regularly took the fall for their men through elaborate schemes that would keep their husbands out of jail. Before the 1990s, authorities often saw through that but had little faith that mafia wives or daughters had the intellect or courage to cooperate in such schemes of their own volition. So women were often given lighter sentences and a chance to testify against their husbands, though few ever did.

Yet, time and again, even today, male authors and mafia experts write that women cannot belong to the groups because they don't take part in the traditional rituals of entry, even though they are demonstrably very much part of these groups, conducting business, running families, and acting as complicit confidantes to the most powerful bosses. The blindness of the mafia's misogyny in failing to recognize the contributions of women strangely seems to give rise to an equal blindness in those tasked with making sense of the mafia's rigidly codified history. And it is just that—history.

"Criminal organizations are changing," mafia analyst Ernesto Savona of the Catholic University of Milan says, making them "more appealing" to women. "They're producing less violence. They're transforming the hierarchical organization into a more flexible one. That means you'll get more women having managerial roles. We call them 'sweet criminal organizations.'"

Savona's point—that mafia organizations now rely on women because they need secretaries rather than killers— reveals that the blindness of misogyny runs deep. The derogatory take suggests that women are no more considered equals in cruelty than they are in intellect. That women who order heinous deaths and brutal maimings, and mastermind torture of unthinkable savagery are still considered "sweet" falls in line with the patriarchal nature of Italy, where sexism is accepted from the halls of power to the playgrounds. There are no exceptions. Pope Francis, an Argentinian born to Italian parents, who leads the second most influential organization in Italy after the mafia, made headlines when he invited female theologians to a conference not long after he was elected pope, only to call them the "cherries on the cake" when asked about their contributions. Silvio Berlusconi, well-known for his misogynist spectacles, once told an international conference that they should invest in Italy because of the "beautiful secretaries" and once asked the country's minister of equal opportunity—a former topless model he appointed to the role—to marry him during a parliamentary session, seemingly forgetting he was already married. It's often a maddening place to be female, knowing that many, many men truly do not believe you can do a job as well (or better) than they can.

Cerreti made clear to me just how well mafia women really do measure on the scale of brutality. Women, she explained, are far crueler than men when it comes to enacting vendettas, and their judgments seem to be less filtered through established criminal conventions. "Even when they have no direct role in a murder, it is often the woman who suggests that the children of someone who has betrayed the family be killed," she says. They think about things differently, they know exactly what will hurt someone the most.

Roberto Saviano's views of women are perhaps the most often quoted. "Apart from a few rare exceptions, the mafiosa exists only in relation to her man," he told *Vice* in an interview in 2015. "Without him, she's like an inanimate being—only half a person. That's why mob wives appear so unkempt and disheveled when accompanying their men to court—it's a cultivated look meant to underscore their fidelity."

Saviano has also told the story of Immacolata Capone, a Camorra woman who rose through the ranks and was killed for it in 2004. He wrote recently that while the police "never discovered a motive for the murder," he surmised that it had to have been because "the clans may not have appreciated her attempt to climb the ranks. Her fierce ambition may have frightened them, and given her business acumen, she might have even attempted to undertake a big deal on her own, independently of the Casalese family." He goes on to applaud her for her strength, as if the characteristic was rare in a female. "The only thing we know for sure is that Capone had successfully navigated the pressures, limitations, and expectations put on women to leave her mark on mob history."

There are few women with a stronger will to fight back than Maria Angela Di Trapani,⁵ the forty-nine-year-old wife of Sicilian Mafia kingpin and serial beheader Salvatore "dagli occhi di ghiaccio" (Salvino eyes of ice) Madonia, who was arrested in Sicily in 2017. Maria Angela took over the organization when her husband was handed down consecutive life sentences. He died in prison in 2007 and was defiant until the end. While it took a few anti-mafia agents to apprehend him at the height of his notoriety, it took two hundred armed police, five special canine units, and several helicopters to make sure Maria Angela didn't get away. It was soon all too clear that while her husband was in jail and with longtime boss of bosses Totò Riina freshly in his grave, she was in charge of reorganizing the entire Sicilian Cosa Nostra. The court documents read something like a *Godfather* screenplay, with several witnesses saying "she acts like a real man," and that her punishments of errant foot soldiers and foes alike were far more vicious than those doled out by most of her male criminal peers.

Women can be charged under Italy's Article 41-bis law, as Trapani was, which allows strict sentences for "mafia association" unless the accused become pentiti, or as Ceretti prefers to call them, collaborators of justice because "they are rarely penitent." The state recognizes them as mafia members even if their own mafia organizations do not. And while many women have unarguable power, they still cannot come into that power without a man allowing them to do so.

When I put the question about equality to Pupetta, she was coy. "Women most certainly know their roles and how to best work the system," she said. Pupetta was more succinct about those who betray her or the system she was so much a part of. She kept what she described as a "detailed diary" of the events of her life, written in dialect. It contains a long list of those who betrayed her. "Not a hit list," she told me when I asked, though every deed for which she is publicly known was built on avenging betrayals.

To say I was worried that she would see my telling of her story as a betrayal is an understatement. I was in France with a friend the day she died, spending a relaxing New Year's weekend exploring the Loire Valley. Suddenly my phone blew up with messages, calls, emails. "Pupetta is dead," most said, sending me Italian news links. Claire Longrigg called me for an interview for a story she was writing. She was the first English-speaking journalist to interview Pupetta. I was the last. To say I didn't feel a sense of relief about her death would be a lie. I felt at once appreciative that I had the opportunity to get to know this woman and sad that she had died, but overwhelmingly I was relieved that Lady Camorra couldn't come after me.

Cristina Pinto, a curly-haired Neapolitan brunette whose teeth have been worn thin at the roots by years of chain-smoking, perfectly affects her nickname, Nikita, after the assassin in Luc Besson's 1990 film *La Femme Nikita*. Pinto served twenty-three years of a thirty-year sentence for crimes she doesn't exactly deny committing as the head of a female motorcycle gang that acted as bodyguards to a powerful Camorra boss named Mario Perrella. By having women lead his trained assassins, Perrella often escaped capture because authorities didn't suspect they were protecting him. And because the women were not thought to be in charge, they often escaped prosecution if they were found lying for him or hiding him. Nikita tells of essentially interviewing for the job. "The competition was fierce among the women, one as tough as the next, we were all trying to outdo each other, to be the worst," she said. "I gave it my best and he chose me."

Nikita was trained as a sharpshooter at the age of seventeen. Later, she and her fellow bodyguards underwent brutal training in what amounted to a boot camp where each was taught a special skill, from weapons assembly to car mechanics. Her childhood had been difficult; her father beat her and police records suggest she was sexually assaulted by several family members. Now, at the age of forty-nine, she works on a fishing boat in the town of Pozzuoli, a few miles north of Naples. Pozzuoli, home to Italy's primary women's prison now that Poggioreale's female-only section is closed, is a rough town by any standard of measure, and its prison a crime school every bit as successful in turning out seasoned criminals as its predecessor. It is the gateway to the Via Domitiana, a stretch of Camorra-controlled highway where thousands of Nigerian migrant women have been trafficked for sex by factions of the Nigerian mafia[6] and the Camorra for years.

The area where Nikita feels most at home is the Campi Flegrei, or Phlegraean Fields, also called the burning fields. It is one of the largest supervolcanoes in the world, which periodically rumbles, causing the rise and fall of the terrain. Buildings have deep vertical fissures from the earth's moving crust, and the main square has a sunken garden with pillars that are marked by stains from the rising soil and sea level over the centuries. Nikita dismisses the danger of living in a place that could erupt with little notice as nothing short of symbolic. She shows me scars on the sunken walls of the port where the water level has left its mark and I can't help but think she sees herself in the same way: scarred, strong, and a survivor.

Nikita does not give interviews after what she calls "bad press" from a TV movie in 2018 that painted her as a lesbian tomboy and launched her to a cult-like notoriety. "I dissociated myself in order to start my life again," she says when I try to prompt her to reflect on her violent youth. "I do not think with hindsight; it is useless to wonder if today I would do things differently."

But she will engage in conversations if you help with the fishing nets.

Her hands are rough and calloused from the fishing work, and her auburn curls are badly dyed and tied back with a pink scrunchie like you'd see on a child. She says fishing keeps her out of jail, though police records show that her boat is often stopped and searched by police looking for contraband.

She was arrested in 1992 on her way into hiding with her three-year-old daughter, a child who resulted from a secret affair with a clansman. After a hit ordered by Perrella went terribly wrong, the crime boss was arrested and decided to collaborate with authorities. He subsequently threw Nikita and the other women under the bus, telling investigators that while, yes, he had paid them to carry out the murder, Nikita could have refused but instead led her gang of women into battle.

The second condition of my conversation with Nikita, in which I was neither allowed nor able to take notes due to the untangling of the slimy nets, was that I not discuss Perrella, of whom she seemed oddly protective. It seems perhaps counterintuitive for a journalist to agree on allowable topics in an interview, but it is often easier to go deeper on the subjects that remain in play if you agree to the boundaries. I have met so many criminals who, despite their lives being part of extensive dossiers and court cases, are hyperprotective of their privacy. Part of it is undoubtedly a desperate desire for control over lives spun out of control; but I always feel that the bigger issue is an attempt to control or even rewrite the narrative. Mixing and mingling with liars and villains hardens one to what the real truth is.

But almost every lie I've been told as part of my crime reporting contains some truth. Nikita is perhaps one of the most skilled interviewees I have ever spoken with. She presents as paranoid, but she is actually in total control of the conversation at all times. She has what seem to be rehearsed movements, a flip of her super curly hair and the raising of one eyebrow don't strike me as entirely spontaneous. I wondered even if they are signals of some sort. At one point as we were at work on the dock, I was convinced someone was watching us, and she was sending them signals with her movements. Other fishermen seemed to ignore her intentionally—perhaps too much so.

Without taking notes, it is hard to quote Nikita directly from our day at the dock. She discussed being part of the motorcycle gang as a decoy for police who would have thought they were just a female riding club, telling me they were among the few who wore helmets on Italian roads before a helmet law came into effect in 1999. They did it not for their safety but so they couldn't be identified. They were also all trained by a skilled assassin who would berate them if they couldn't shoot and hit the bull's-eye painted onto posters of anti-mafia judges. But one thing she said is forever emblazoned into my mind. "Don't for a minute mistake women who fear they will be killed for a simple misstep as weak," she told me. "There is no way someone outside this world would ever understand the courage it takes to stay." It was the first time I had heard it put that way. Usually people who have left organized crime groups talk about the courage to leave.

I first met Nikita at an International Investigative Journalism conference in 2016 when she was a keynote speaker around a docudrama that featured her unusual life. She told the audience about how she was inducted into Perrella's "family" by being handed a .38 caliber pistol when she was just twenty-two. She clarified that the two were never lovers, as had been rumored for years. "I liked his way of doing things," she said. "When he talked about the Camorra his eyes lit up."

He also saw something in her and hired her immediately, she said. "I was already known in the criminal circles, there was no ceremony for the oath, those are things that the 'Ndrangheta does not the Camorra," she said. "Mario put that .38 caliber and 500,000 lire in my hand, which in a few days became one million a week."

She was mesmerizing as she spoke about her choice to join this elite band of killers as if she were discussing becoming the CEO of a business. She was less convincing when she described her decision to change her life. Ultimately, after hemming and hawing about what drove her decision to leave the Camorra when she got out of prison, she first said it was for her daughter, who was just three when she was placed into custody. Then she expressed her disappointment in the group. "The Camorra isn't like it used to be," she said. "They were all very different than what I was expecting. I was hoping there would be a complicity, a higher form of friendship, even loyalty. I was expecting too much from them, so I had to leave."

She says she left the Camorra without having to collaborate with anti-mafia prosecutors. She says, "fortunately they let me go," and held no grudge or remorse. "None of my family have had to suffer extortion or pay a price for me leaving," she said, which is wholly incredible given the long history of those who could only leave organized crime groups in a coffin. It's hard not to think she might still have one foot in the clubhouse, but I dared not ask her directly.

Covering crime often means developing a somewhat skewed view of good and evil. In the case of someone like Nikita—whose rap sheet includes arms procurement, kidnapping, and organizing more than a dozen murders, including the death of an eleven-year-old boy—those of us in the audience when she spoke at the journalism festival couldn't help but be starstruck. The first time I felt this sensation of being totally mesmerized by listening to the confessions of a very bad person was early on in my career when I covered the case of Elisabeth Fritzl, who was repeatedly raped by her father, Josef, who kept her in a dungeon. Her father eventually confessed to rape, slavery, and murdering one of the eight children he fathered in the twenty-four years he kept his daughter captive. As his confession played out in the courtroom in Sankt Poelten, Austria, many people held their hands over their ears or covered their faces. The crime journalists in the room instead could not get enough of the details.

Covering crime is never about the actual assault, murder, or beating—it is about the psyche behind these transgressive acts. People like Fritzl and Nikita offer a window into the mind of such a sick person, a view that helps unravel the story and makes us better storytellers, though it is arguable that we who do this for a living are in some way scarred by it.

Nikita's talk was haunting in the way she normalized such blatant criminality, and her conversation on the pier with me was candid, though I dare not believe it was totally honest. She described her life as Perrella's armed guard, in charge of both guarding him physically but also in arranging the logistical details behind attacks he carried out. "I had my own group, we were four," she said. "Everyone was dealing with a specific thing: drugs, weapons, settling of scores."

Perrella inspired Nikita by telling her he wanted to read about her work in the newspapers, which served to push her to make him proud. "When I shot, I felt even more powerful than I wanted to feel," she explained. "We were trained, like soldiers, when you are in the Camorra you change everything about you: the way you speak, move, behave."

By the end of her talk, she had come around to understand how badly she had been misled. "When you are part of a criminal group, you have the feeling of being stronger and stronger, but you don't realize that that power is never yours," she said. But despite admitting fully her involvement in the Camorra and its various crimes, she fervently denies ever being a boss or even in charge of the other militant guards, insisting that the idea of female mafiosi is a joke. She says women who were given "temporary power" when their husbands or brothers went to jail squandered the opportunity to be true leaders. "They are like children," she says. "Untrained and undisciplined."

I asked Nikita about Pupetta, to which she said simply, "That was a brave woman. She did a man's job."

Though they almost always deny having attained power, these women's drive to reach the upper echelon of criminal syndicates is clear. I often think back to my Italian friend who advised me that the only way to combat the sexism was to ignore it or harness it, that by flying under the radar one could make much more ground.

An anti-mafia investigator in Naples told me the best example he had seen of a mafia woman's relentless ambition to succeed was the story of Teresa De Luca Bossa,[7] who is serving multiple sentences for the activities she signed off on as a Camorra clan boss.

Teresa came to power after her brother, a Camorra boss, was imprisoned. Teresa's time at the helm was fruitful for the clan. She was able to bury the hatchet with a rival clan and carry out lucrative deals for the group, which won her accolades, expanding her clan to become one of the Camorra's most powerful.

After a brief stint in jail during which she made valuable contacts, Teresa escaped and hid out with 'Ndrangheta friends in Calabria, giving orders to her clan from there even as police started closing in. She was arrested in 2010 in the swimming pool of a luxury glamping spot in southern Campania near the ancient ruins of Paestum. The undercover police were dressed in bikinis and Speedos and posed as tourists.

Teresa was the first woman to be sentenced under the Article 41-bis legislation for mafia crimes, meaning even the investigators recognized her power, in stark contrast to historical cases when they thought women couldn't possibly have climbed the criminal ladder. Three years later, Teresa's daughter, Anna, who had filled the power vacuum after her mother's arrest, survived an assassination attempt after a hit man pumped seven bullets into her pelvis and thighs. Anna's oldest son had been murdered by a rival gang and Anna had intended to carry out the vendetta personally—Pupetta style. She was even caught on a wiretap invoking Pupetta's name, and ultimately lived up to the example of the woman who inspired her. After Anna's wounds healed, she was sentenced to life in prison for her role in the double homicide of two rival clansmen who killed her son, which she is believed to have ordered from her hospital bed.

Teresa and Anna both denied true clan involvement and have courted the press incessantly, giving prison interviews that cite the fact that since women cannot be inducted into the criminal group, the prosecutors exhibited unfairness in trying them for mafia-affiliation crimes. If they aren't allowed to be officially part of the mafia, how can they be charged as mafia women?

Pupetta dismissed and confirmed her own involvement at the same time. She kept a scrapbook of yellowed newspaper clippings about the crimes she and those close to her committed. She had hundreds about her trial for the murder of Antonio Esposito, the man who ordered the hit on her husband when they were newlyweds—and whom she readily admitted killing when she was just eighteen years old and pregnant. "People used to send these to me," she told me of the clippings as she leafed through them. "I don't know why I keep them," she then said, smiling, making it clear why she did.

A moment later she lit a cigarette and adamantly denied details of her life as reported in the thousands of press accounts written about her. She ranted about how journalists have wronged her over the years, even though she has been one of the most accessible "falsely imprisoned" women in Italy. She admitted to murdering Esposito but remained defiant about her prison sentence. "I should have never served a day in jail for that after he destroyed my family," she said, appearing to forget, at least for a moment, that she had remained with the father of her other children long after he was thought to have killed the son she had with Pasqualone.

The fact remains that Pupetta was an attention seeker. She has appeared in films, called into radio and television programs, and in her younger days even held press conferences when local reporters got it "wrong" about her family members or when her rivals were given a pass. And as she sat with me during my earliest visits, I couldn't help wonder what she hoped to get out of it.

"Americans haven't written much about me," she told me. "They might be interested." In fact, news of her death was reported all over the world. "Lady Camorra," the "first female crime boss," was dead. Some stories wildly exaggerated her power and influence, but I know she would have loved it, carefully clipping and placing each article about her in her scrapbook.

4

Sex and Honor

Pupetta once described sex appeal and the use of blatant flir-
tation as a sort of flammable oil that makes tricky situations
go smoother, but that can ultimately blow up and turn deadly.

While the riddling of Antonio Esposito with twenty-nine bullets in a public space was a horrific crime, there was something
terribly sexy about Pupetta's act of vengeance. It wasn't so much
the love and devotion to Pasqualone that drove her to carry out
the vendetta that people—especially Umberto—admired. It
was that she had the balls to do it at a time when women were
seen as weak and incapable. The female yearning for equality
and sexual freedom that was bubbling under the surface in the
United States at the time never fully reached Italy, and certainly
in the 1950s, a woman carrying out such a brazen murder as
Pupetta did—while pregnant—was seen as astonishing. It was
also inspiring to many younger women who were watching
their peers elsewhere in the world escape the miseries inflicted

on them by abusive men, and who wished they, too, had what it took to carry out such an act, especially against men who were abusing them.

At the time Pupetta committed her first murder, men in Italy were permitted by law to carry out honor killings if their wife betrayed them. It wouldn't be until the 1990s that murder inspired by a *raptus*—the Latin word for "seized," often referring to jealousy caused by the woman's blatant action—was outlawed. Rarely is a man's lack of control over his feelings of ownership of a woman mentioned. Even in 2021, femicide in Italy is rampant, with one woman murdered by a man she had previously loved every three days. In December 2020, a seventy-year-old man was absolved from murdering his sixty-two-year-old wife, who was a high school teacher in the northern town of Brescia. The judge ruled that he had suffered a delirio di gelosia, "delirium of jealousy," over her young male students. The judge felt he was mentally incapacitated by his jealous rage and thus forgiven for taking his wife's life. According to court documents, he first knocked her out cold with a rolling pin and then slit her throat.

Rarely do women take their own form of revenge, and when they do, they are described as hysterical. Pupetta was ahead of her time in many ways, acting as few women have felt empowered to do until recently. There are those exceptions, like Nikita whose fearlessness was admirable, but it has taken women in crime circles a long time to even reach the glass ceiling.

The Italian director Francesco Rosi saw the artistic potential of Pupetta's strength—albeit admittedly misguided by the standards of civilized society. He memorialized her story in his late

1950s film *La Sfida*, which roughly translates to *The Challenge*. The role of Pupetta was played by the siren of the moment, Rosanna Schiaffino, a cover model who went on to make forty-five largely forgettable movies. The film won the Jury Prize at the Venice Film Festival in 1958, around the time Pupetta's infamy was reaching its peak. Even the movie poster shows the actress playing Pupetta in a sort of Anita Ekberg–esque pout. It was a risky attempt to glamorize Pupetta's brazen act of violence, and it worked. It also underscores just how normalized the mafia has long been in Italy.

Unlike popular American shows like *The Sopranos* and even the *Godfather* trilogy, which glamorized the mob as a fictional set of characters, in Italy the characters are real people you might pass at a grocery store or stand next to at a coffee bar. Even in Pupetta's betrayal, she seemed like the woman next door, because for many she was.

Italians largely view the mafia and the malavita, "dishonest lifestyle," it produces as just another facet of the culture. They have learned to coexist with it rather than see it as a faction of Italian life that has nothing to do with them. It is no stretch to say that every single Italian has in some way rubbed shoulders with someone involved in organized crime, whether knowingly or not. When the stepson of a well-known mobster from the local Roman mob was accepted to my sons' private international school, everyone whispered behind his back and, more tellingly, recalled the various other mobster children who had attended the school in the past, including one whose father was on trial for murder in Sicily during the boy's senior year. Rather than using it as a teaching tool, the administration reportedly made sure no one talked about it or brought newspapers to school to avoid embarrassing him.

The success of the film gave Pupetta the acting bug and she endeavored to audition for screen roles. For a time, she dreamed of being a film star of the caliber of Sophia Loren. Born Sofia Villani Scicolone in Rome before adopting the stage name Sophia Loren, the Italian starlet is the same age as Pupetta and moved to Pozzuoli, where the women's crime school prison is now located, outside of Naples as an infant, after her father refused to marry her mother.

Pupetta would never find acting success, and certainly not on the scale of the legendary Loren, even though she later sang a song she wrote in prison in a cameo appearance in the largely unsuccessful 1967 film *Delitto a Posillipo* and tried her hand acting in a couple of other disastrous productions. Her film career was short-lived, and after a few bad reviews that never quite managed to separate her appeal from her criminal past, she gave it up.

"It was fun, but it wasn't real life," she said of that time. She pulled out another scrapbook and paged through the many newspaper reviews of *La Sfida* and other articles praising her for what was described by some as an extraordinary singing talent and by others as a dismal attempt to exploit her criminal reputation.

There is a tragic insecurity that many faded beauties share, and Pupetta furrowed her painted-on eyebrows at the memory of how truly great she felt her life once was. She never shied away from bragging about her popularity among young mafiosi, either. "I had so many different men trying to visit me at one time, I had to make bookings," she said. "Imagine that!"

Years later, in 1982, Pupetta seemed to have given up her criminal streak, save a murder conviction for the offing of the shady shrink and an investigation into another murder involving a rival clansman for which she was eventually cleared. Still, interest in her story remained strong and the late dictator Benito Mussolini's then-nineteen-year-old granddaughter, Alessandra (who was herself a far-right member of the European Parliament until 2019, when she resigned after her husband was accused of being a patron to underage prostitutes in Rome) played Pupetta in a controversial made-for-TV film called *Il Caso Pupetta Maresca,* or *The Case of Pupetta Maresca.* The small-screen flick angered Pupetta, and she fought bitterly—and successfully—to stop it from airing, in part because she didn't want to be played by a Mussolini, which she argued in court was "an affront to her honor."

With Pupetta's legal battles exhausted and the statutes of limitation running out, the film was set to air in 1994 on Italy's state broadcaster RAI. Pupetta again dispatched her curiously abundant lawyers on the producers. This time she was joined by Alessandra Mussolini herself, who had by then launched her political career and didn't want a film in which she played a notorious mafiosa to damage her hard-fought reputation. At the time, Mussolini—whose aunt is none other than Sophia Loren—was having a hard enough time trying to navigate a scandal tied to the August 1983 edition of Italian *Playboy* magazine, in which she had posed nude for the cover and centerfold.

Such was the place Pupetta inhabited in the Italian public's imagination that the politician worried her portrayal of the mafia woman twelve years earlier would give her political enemies more ammunition to use against her than would the publication of her nude photos, a more egregious affront to public morality in the 1990s than it might be considered today.

In 2013, another made-for-TV film garnered an entirely different reception. *Pupetta: The Courage and the Passion* was released without incident, and Pupetta even cooperated with the publicity, posing on the film set with Manuela Arcuri, the tall, thin actress who portrayed her murdering Antonio Esposito.[1] "Think about what I went through then, that I really shot, what I thought at that moment, the blind terror, my trembling hands, I was hidden behind the car. I was sure they would kill me," Pupetta said in an interview tied to the release. "Manuela found my spirit, she embodied the passion of that moment in my life perfectly."

What Pupetta undoubtedly liked most about Manuela's portrayal of her was the starlet's raw sex appeal, which she wielded like a weapon. Pupetta once described sex appeal and the use of blatant flirtation as a sort of flammable oil that makes tricky situations go more smoothly, but that can ultimately blow up and turn deadly. When Pupetta died, Arcuri drew scorn for honoring her in an Instagram post that was later removed, in which she called Pupetta a "courageous, strong, fearless woman" who "acted impetuously" and sometimes "made mistakes."

In the 1950s and '60s, there was no sexual revolution in Italy. Instead, the Catholic Church was clamping down on sex outside of marriage even as women in the rest of the world were burning bras, popping birth control pills, and exploring their sexuality. In Italy, the pill was introduced in the late 1960s, but pharmacies were not authorized to sell it. Abortion became legal in 1978, but many hospitals and doctors affiliated with the Vatican still refuse to perform the procedure. As a result, sex in Italy for Pupetta's generation came only with the promise of marriage. She insisted she had never had a one-night stand or slept with anyone she did not truly and wholly love at the time. "It's wrong to do that," she said. "Young women today just give their pussies away for free, without thought to the power they can have."

The absurd sexual morality in mafia organizations has always been tied to the sense of religious devotion to which many of the most notorious criminals faithfully adhere. Sigmund Freud's Madonna-whore complex perfectly captures how this attitude translates into the mafia's treatment of women— women are thought of only as holy Madonna figures or sluts, never both and nothing in between. Mafia experts often describe top bosses as pious, having "conservative sex" with their wives as a form of respect, saving the more adventurous interludes for their lovers or prostitutes (even as it is also often said that a real mafioso will never have to spend a penny for sex), a description shared by journalist Girolamo Lo Verso, who parsed the Sicilian mafia mentality in his 2017 book *The Mafia Psychopathology*.

The Sicilian proverb "Cummannari è meglio di futtiri" (Commanding is better than fucking) is a long-held adage, according to Lo Verso, who says that the risk that an emotional attachment could lead to compromise or weakness is far too great to allow long-running extramarital affairs. "Sexuality in this world is generally limited to fleeting sexual relations with wives and the company of women of loose morals as an external show of virility," he says.[2] "The mafioso must respect his wife—who is fundamentally sexually repressed—which means that he must have no other public relationships. This means that the power over life and death held by Cosa Nostra is more important than erotic-affective relationships."

Like so many other Italianisms that seep from normal society into the underworld, infidelity is hard to avoid. The popular saying "non c'è due senza tre" (in two there are always three)—said with a wink—implies that all enduring coupledoms survive only because of lovers who keep them from getting bored with their spouses. Across all the syndicates, women take lovers, too—though at a much greater risk than their husbands.

In 2016, a Cosa Nostra kingpin named Mariano Marchese ordered the brutal beating to death of an unfaithful mafia wife whose much-older husband had just gone to prison for life for the usual crimes of murder, coersion, and collusion. Police intercepted a number of phone calls between the seventy-six-year-old cuckolded husband and Marchese and his associates as they hashed out what they should do to his much-younger wife after discovering she had taken up with a local barista who had nothing to do with the crime syndicate but who would have clearly known who she was married to. "She is showing a lack of respect to all of us," Marchese was heard telling those he tasked with her murder on a wiretap that was released to the press by investigators. "It's a question of respect for our dignity."

Police intervened when they overheard Marchese give the marching orders to carry out the young wife's murder. "I want her in a room and beaten with wooden sticks," he directed them. "Her brains smashed open." The woman went on to seek protection, though she is not known to have testified against her husband or any of his associates.

Another particularly unfaithful mafia wife named Angela Bartucca is often referred to in police records as a "femme fatale." While she survived any retribution from her 'Ndrangheta husband, who was sentenced to a lengthy prison term, she was ultimately connected to the deaths of several of the young lovers she took when her husband was incarcerated.

Her first was handcuffed inside the car he and Angela had used to secretly meet for sex. The vehicle was set on fire while he was still alive in it. A second lover's bruised and bloodied corpse was tied to a tree under which he once engaged in a romantic tryst with Angela, according to a turncoat who, at the time, was given the job of spying on her, and who also told investigators that the lover was beaten to death slowly over a number of days with ample attention to his genitalia, which had, in part, been dismembered. A third and final lover was Valentino Galati, a younger 'Ndrangheta man who was sent to guard her and keep her from cheating. Not long after his assignment started, the two ended up in bed. Valentino disappeared— another traceless lupara bianca death.

In some rare cases, especially when the husband is much older than the wife and has been sentenced to life, he will consent to a proxy for the sake of her sexual needs. This ensures her own survival in case she dares to try to find someone on her own. In many cases, the local priest is called in for the job, since he will never commit to falling in love with her.

While mafia men seem, at least in public, to prefer their women angelic, mafia women seem to keenly understand the power of their sexuality. For those who are incarcerated, a few coquettish glances can easily soften up the male guards, which often leads to a little extra time in the rec yard or even gifts from outside. Pupetta used her own seductive gifts with great mastery, often winning favors for other inmates as well, who would then owe her.

On the outside, provocative conversation can be used to test alliances and elicit secrets. Many mafiosi daughters and sisters have been coaxed into using their sex appeal against the enemy. Throughout the history of Italy's major syndicates, legend states that confiding in a woman was often seen as a grave betrayal, punishable by death in certain cases. The idea was that if a woman could get a man to break the omertà, she might also get him to turn on his criminal brethren in other ways, or even to the police. Pupetta whispered to me in her kitchen about a woman she knew whose sole job was coaxing secrets out of rival clansmen. "She paid a huge price for it because once she was discovered, they sliced off her breasts and let her bleed to death," she told me without wincing.

Still, while it plays into a certain romantic image of the loyal mafia wife to think of her crying alone in bed until her husband returns smelling of his lovers' perfume, there is ample evidence to suggest that the wives are also playing around on the side.

Today, mafia women are often key confidantes to their men, going far beyond just filling in when they are incarcerated and instead acting as key advisers who can easily step in when they need to. Because of the intimacy of this bond, betrayal becomes even more dangerous. Anti-mafia prosecutor Cerreti took a calculated risk when she successfully lured Maria Concetta Cacciola, a woman born into one of the most violent factions of the 'Ndrangheta whose own destiny seemed sealed by fate, to the state's side. Maria Concetta's mother, Anna Rosalba Lazzaro, was deeply involved in her family's 'ndrine, and her father, Michele Cacciola, was himself a top-tier boss. Maria Concetta lived an unenviable life from a young age, during which she had expressed a desire to leave Calabria and all the crime and corruption that were wrong with it. Instead, her father married her off to rival Salvatore Antonio Figliuzzi at the age of thirteen to settle a vendetta, and she was systematically beaten and raped by her husband for years. She later described a personal hell of violence, fear, oppression, and cruelty that often included her husband holding his pistol to her forehead and pulling the trigger on a gun; she had no idea whether it was loaded.

Her husband eventually went to jail for mafia-related crimes, during which Maria Concetta filed for divorce and had the audacity to start a new relationship. Her family publicly scorned her actions, reminding her that marriage is for life and the only way out is death. She was eventually held hostage by her father and locked up and beaten in her childhood home until she promised to leave her new lover and stay devoted to her imprisoned husband.

On May 11, 2011, at the age of thirty-one and with her husband set to serve several more years in prison, she decided to leave once and for all. She had been summoned to the local police station after her son Alfonso had been stopped for driving without a license. At that moment, she spontaneously told a police officer that she wanted to talk to someone about her experience, including her family.

The head of the precinct called Cerreti, who told them to tell Maria Concetta to go back home and pretend that nothing was wrong, in order to avoid arousing suspicion. Even the slightest delay at a police station in the heart of 'Ndrangheta country could prove fatal. She'd be killed by her own parents if for any reason they thought she might turn into a pentita, and Cerreti didn't want that to happen. The police told her to come back a week later.

The delay served two purposes. If Maria Concetta was serious about confessing her role and testifying against her family, she would come back. If instead she had been sent to try to get something from police or lay a trap, she wouldn't return. A week later, Cerreti was waiting with local police in the Rosarno station when Maria Concetta walked through the side door. She went back twice more, and on May 25, after Cerreti was able to corroborate some of what Concetta had told her, she decided it was time to put Maria Concetta into protective custody. Under Italian law, police then have just 180 days to work with the collaborators to try to get as much corroborated information as they can to extend protective custody. Often that's not enough time, which puts the turncoats at risk. It's a flaw in the judicial system that crime families are well aware of, and they do what they can to trip up police work if they suspect someone has given evidence. Cerreti would like to see the time limit extended. "We have a short period of time to understand the entire situation," Cerreti told me. And even once protection is granted, it is reevaluated every four years to determine whether the collaborator is still cooperative, has returned to the mafia family, or has disappeared.

The stories Maria Concetta told police were astonishing, offering a horrific inside view of life deep inside the labyrinth of the 'Ndrangheta's complicated structure. She unveiled the complex relationship between her parents' crime families, introducing a number of people law enforcement had never considered to be such integral players. By the end of May, she was living safely on the other side of Italy under an assumed name, but she knew that the 'Ndrangheta would never forget—or forgive— her betrayal. Further, her children were still back in Calabria, and they were being used in what amounted to a blackmail campaign to get her to rescind her confession.

Through a trustworthy contact, Maria Concetta started sending messages back home to stay apprised of her children's welfare. She was assured they weren't doing well in her absence. The contact, who was likely not trustworthy, said they were being abused for her "crimes" against the family. With each message, Maria Concetta grew more desperate, pleading with Cerreti to somehow get her children out of there, which proved impossible. With her husband in prison and the children living with family members, there was no legal reason to remove them. Italian law works to protect collaborators, but for those who risk their lives to escape their abusive and criminal existence, the loopholes are frustrating—or worse.

On August 2, 2011, just three months after she turned, and

after hearing that her children were near the breaking point, Maria Concetta reached out directly to her mother and brother, despite having given police ample evidence against both of them. Even if she knew it would be a fatal decision, she wanted to hug her children one more time.

The family made a plan to pick her up from her hiding place, which at that time was in Genoa. They promised her they would allow her to hold all three of her children and return to safety, explaining that they "understood" why she fled. At the last minute, Maria Concetta got scared and called the police, who intervened before her family could collect her from Genoa.

Maria Concetta's family wouldn't give up, and they pressured her to return home, promising her security and offering to hire lawyers to make sure she was safe. She was torn between wanting to see her children and wanting to protect herself, but ultimately she needed to see them again. On August 8, she returned to Rosarno. She hugged her children, and the lawyers she was told were there to protect her instead coaxed her into signing a retraction of her confession, taping what would be the last words she ever spoke.

Three days later, she was dead from drinking muriatic/ hydrochloric acid, which her family said she did to take her life. The coroner's report reads like a horror movie script. She had drunk a liter of the acid, which would have burned her throat and been impossible to do on her own, given that the body's reflexes would have made her vomit. It was as if someone had poured it down her throat. Her official cause of death was a heart attack, undoubtedly prompted by excruciating pain as the acid ate through her esophagus and stomach walls. Still, her family said she had committed suicide for having betrayed the family.

Cerreti did not believe the suicide excuse, citing dozens of "traitors" who had died after clearly being forced to drink acid, a not-so-subtle message to others contemplating betrayals of their own. At least half a dozen 'Ndrangheta women died after drinking acid between 2005 and 2015, according to the local Reggio Calabria death records. Four had tried to confess to police, and the other two had cheated on their 'Ndrangheta husbands.

A few days after her body was found, Maria Concetta's family filed an official complaint against Cerreti and her team, accusing the star anti-mafia prosecutor of coercion and preying on someone with mental-health issues. The complaints followed a convenient script that implies women are too weak-minded to make such decisions on their own. They insisted that prosecutors had coerced the turncoat victim to "fabricate allegations" in exchange for money and security that never came. The family cited tricks by law enforcement they claim were meant to break family bonds by using children as a carrot to get them to confess. That so many turncoats rescind their stories is the best proof yet that leaving an organized-crime syndicate is often fatal—with the exception of Giusy Pesce, who is still alive, at least for the moment.

Cerreti, shaken by what she knew in her heart was the murder of her star witness, ordered an investigation into the death, which eventually found Maria Concetta's father and brother involved in her demise, though only on a peripheral level. In 2014, an appellate court in Reggio Calabria reduced their negligible sentences even further, dropping her father's sentence from five years and four months to four years, and her brother's sentence down from six years to four years and six months. Her mother's two-year sentence was upheld.

Still, Maria Concetta's ultimate sacrifice for the truth did not stop Cerreti from seeking out the next brave woman who could help her kneecap the 'Ndrangheta. While working with Giuseppina Pesce, she received a letter in her office from another Giuseppina who was a distant cousin of her recently deceased star witness.

Giuseppina Multari, who had been under witness protection since 2006, had sent a cryptic note of encouragement through Cerreti to her distant relative. Multari had been forced to marry Antonio Cacciola, Maria Concetta's brother-in-law; he'd abused drugs and frequently abused her in depressive fits of rage. Her husband eventually died by suicide, though Cerreti believes he was killed for betraying his chosen wife. Giuseppina was accused by his family of instigating his depression and blamed entirely for the suicide, and her punishment was to be held captive and raped by whoever craved sex—or power—among his surviving family.

On the night her husband died, she later told investigators, her father-in-law, Salvatore, took her by the arms. "He shakes me and says if my son killed himself for you, I'll kill you and all your family," she said. "From that moment, the situation has become absolutely unlivable for me . . . I could not leave the house freely, only by asking permission from my in-laws or brothers-in-law, who should have accompanied me. No one spoke a word to me. I was also prevented from taking care of myself, in the sense that it was they who determined which doctor and how they should visit me."

Her captors were mostly other women, sisters-in-law who felt no mercy or perhaps envied the fact that Giuseppina's husband had died and thus she no longer had to suffer marital abuse.

The note she wrote to her cousin was a simple one, amounting to, "Good job! Stay strong!" and was signed "G. Multari, Witness Protection."

Intrigued, Cerreti searched the archives to figure out more about this woman she had never met and found the records buried in layers of forgotten bureaucracy. She learned how Multari had been kept as a tortured slave by her husband's family. Each night her captors locked her and her three daughters in their home and then kept her segregated from others by day, unable to leave the home except to take her three children to school or visit her dead husband's grave. Their reasons for keeping her under constant guard are not entirely clear, as Cerreti is vague about why Multari was such a prized possession.

One night in 2006, Multari's captors had gone to a party and she climbed out of a window and ran to the busy seaside, hoping she could blend in until she found someone who could help her. Her brother, also part of the group who terrorized her, tracked her down. He took her to the hospital and said his gift to her was not returning her home. But when authorities refused to help her, citing lack of proof that she was sincere about leaving, she found herself back in her captive hell. Eventually, she wrote a letter to the local DDA (Direzione Distrettuale Antimafia, or National Anti-Mafia Directorate) and left it with a teacher at her children's school, hoping she would send it. The letter explained her situation and that of her children, giving intricate details about various 'ndrine members and the address where she could be found. The police rescued her and her kids and put them in protective custody, which soon became a new kind of prison.

No one ever came to take her testimony or to explain what was supposed to happen next, until Cerreti reached out to her six years after she had gone underground. "There was no reason this woman, whose life was such hell, was forgotten like this," Cerreti said. "I was sure she had a credible story to tell if only because she was still waiting and had not dared to go back."

What Giuseppina Multari told Cerreti led to the discovery of one of the biggest stolen weapons caches ever found in Europe and the arrest of sixteen bosses in Calabria, Germany, and the Netherlands under the Deus investigation who were eventually convicted of mafia collusion with the intent to infiltrate European Union–funded entities. Her testimony also led to the arrest of every single member of the Rizziconi town council for organized crime and the city government to be dissolved.

After Cerreti secured the arrests of the arms traffickers, she turned her focus on those who had kept Giuseppina and her children captive for so long. By the end of Cerreti's investigation, the torturers were arrested and charged under ancient antislavery legislation that had not been invoked for decades. The convictions included three women: forty-three-year-old Maria

Cacciola, thirty-six-year-old Jessica Oppedisano, and sixty-three-year-old Teresa D'Agostino, who are still in prison at the time of this writing.

Mario Puzo's 1969 bestselling novel, *The Godfather*, gave armchair crime buffs and mafia aficionados permission to lionize the mob and, in doing so, try to dissect what life is really like inside the deadly underworld. Puzo, who died in 1999, often insisted that his creative account of the Sicilian Cosa Nostra was "purely fictional" and that he had no help from "the inside" when telling his tales with such stunning accuracy. Most who know the story of the real-life mob have little doubt that in making such a claim he was protecting his sources and, very likely, his own skin.

Much of what he wrote about (and what he helped Francis Ford Coppola bring to life for the movie series) rings painfully true, especially his portrayal of women as conservative and somewhat transactional figures. The trilogy aptly portrayed what mafia women were allowed to do during the eras it represents, but so many film depictions that followed Coppola's trilogy get it so wrong.

Blatant promiscuity on the part of mafia women is one of the most commonly misrepresented facets of mafia life in pop culture. Mafia wives and girlfriends tend to be portrayed as provocatively dressed and garishly unsophisticated along the lines of Michele Pfeiffer's bizarre female figure in *Married to the Mob* or the "pants suits and double knits" worn by the wives and molls in *Goodfellas*. Badly scripted scenes in those movies evolved into Carmela Soprano's suburban New Jersey housewife chic, complete with gaudy jewelry, garish fingernails, and spray tans. The portrayals make for great entertainment, but the real world is much different.

In reality, mafia women tend to follow styles trending in the larger culture, with one exception: when they are mourning the loss of a husband, father, or brother, their black attire—customary for mourning women even outside crime culture—is accented by red lingerie under their clothing.

When mourning, even older mafia women who no longer tolerate itchy, lacy thongs and push-up bras will exchange their usual garments for red slips and girdles. But this is not a nod to sexuality, as I had presumed when I had first noticed displays of these red undergarments in Neapolitan shop windows. They were not meant to entice husbands and lovers. According to a tradition that is now decades old, they are symbols of a promise to avenge the deaths of their fallen men, a promise made with the color of blood. Pupetta wore red undergarments throughout her prison term, having them sent in from her favorite Neapolitan intimate apparel shop. She never wore them after she hooked up with Umberto, "out of a sign of respect to the father of my other children."

When mafia men are in prison, it has long been held that their wives and girlfriends are strictly prohibited from wearing makeup or even keeping their hair dyed. They are supposedly required to wear frumpy clothing to avoid giving the impression that they are dressing up for another man, or that they have eyes for anyone but their locked-up partners. Any deviance from this practice assumes betrayal, which is punishable by death and enforced by male family members who take on the incarcerated husband's job of controlling his wife. The practice is strictly adhered to in Calabria and to a large extent in Sicily, but Camorra women are far more free-spirited, and in many ways mavericks when it comes to their independence and often glam up even if their men are behind bars.

Not all mafia folklore stands the test of time. It is still said that across all the syndicates, mafia men prefer to marry virgins they've known from childhood or widows of fallen collaborators, though they are said to be far less picky about their lovers. Roberto Saviano, who says his own account of life inside the Neapolitan Camorra in *Gomorrah* was fed by sources inside the clans he infiltrated, has perpetuated the sexual myths of women and organized crime.

Nevertheless, Saviano insists that the mob has not modernized in line with the rest of the West, and certainly not to the extent to allow female sexuality to be seen as a strength or asset. He claims that the strict Catholic mores that have guided so many mafia families for decades remain intact.

But I've talked to many women who live and operate on various levels of criminality, from perpetrators and turncoats to prosecutors and analysts, and I can only conclude that mafia men do like their wives to be inexperienced, but the virgin myth seems outdated. The thought of another living man with a higher ranking or one who is more amply endowed living in the memory of their woman's sexual fantasies may be troubling for many. But in modern times, finding a virgin is not easy or, it seems, necessary.

Whether the woman of interest is a virgin or not, most mafia men marry either within their clan or into a family at the same or higher standing from another affiliate. It is virtually unheard of that someone from one mafia group would marry someone from another syndicate—unless it is a means of brokering a peace deal or a strategy for expanding territory. Either objective makes it vitally important that young women in mafia clans do not follow their hearts.

This strategic approach to marriage is exactly why Pasqualone fell for Pupetta. Her pedigree was perfect: she had grown up in a crime family, but not one that would give his own any competition. Pupetta laughed that off. "We fell in love, we started writing to each other when he was in prison and by the time he got out, the passion had built up," she said, showing me several of his handwritten letters she kept in various boxes separated by categories she simply would not share with me.

Like so many duties that restrict and contain the lives of young mafia women, keeping them from falling in love spontaneously is the responsibility of the girl's own family, primarily her mother, who will tirelessly preach the moral responsibility of keeping the family's "good" reputation intact by refraining from unapproved relationships while somehow instilling in them that all the blood and chaos of the clan's existence is morally acceptable.

Mafiosi fathers also work hard to preserve their daughters' integrity—for the right man of his or the wider clan's choosing. Many a mafia daughter has met her death for daring to choose her own man. In 1983, a pretty twenty-four-year-old named Annunziata Giacobbe, who was the daughter of an 'Ndrangheta underboss, was summoned to the countryside near Rosarno, in Calabria.[3] Afraid to go alone, she asked her eighteen-year-old cousin, Antonio, to go with her, expecting he would protect her. Near the meeting point, the two were jumped by four picciotti, or 'Ndrangheta apprentices, sent on the job to earn credibility to eventually take part in full initiation rites.

The young thugs peppered the cousins with bullets and ran off, but turned back after they heard Annunziata moaning in pain, having somehow survived the initial volley. They promptly slit her throat with a pruning knife and left her for dead. Police determined that the 'Ndrangheta boss Vincenzo Pesce ordered the killing because Annunziata, who was promised from birth to one of his family's sons, had fallen in love with someone else. It was better that she was dead than to shun his son for real love.

The great contradiction, of course, is that mafia sons do as they please. A young man can have as many lovers as he wants before and even after he settles down. A mafia journalist explained to me once that younger wives in the Camorra and the 'Ndrangheta insist their husbands take on foreign lovers, preferring that their men bed down with Russians, Moldovans, or Polish women instead of Italians who might be tied to other clans or in some way cause complications in the wider criminal community. The foreign women would never be true competition, he insisted, either because they are perceived to be socially inferior or because no true mafioso would ever want to risk poisoning the bloodline by introducing an ethnic mix.

I once interviewed an 'Ndrangheta woman who had become the mistress of someone "not approved" by an older male in her family and so was made to suffer the kind of punishment prescribed for a transgression such as hers. The woman, whom I will call Monica, met me in a safe house in Rome after she'd received too many stitches to contemplate for wounds from a particularly brutal gang rape. Monica's arms were covered with cigarette-burn scars of varying degrees of pink, which I took to indicate the wounds were inflicted over a long period of time. She had been caught having an affair with an archenemy of her husband while he was in jail. Monica told me in no uncertain terms that she deserved what she got and that, in retrospect, the rival was likely only interested in her as a means of dishonoring her husband. Her lack of self-esteem struck me as a common thread among mafia women, certainly, but also among many Italian women who have been berated and belittled and made to think they are just sex objects. It is no great secret that Italian machoism has been bolstered for generations because men have been spoon-fed ridiculous portrayals of women in Italian media. I once interviewed a CEO of a company in Milan and couldn't take my eyes off the billboard outside his window of a woman essentially performing fellatio on a Magnum ice cream bar. Subliminal sexism keeps women from advancing. Photos are still required on résumés in Italy, and jobs can advertise age ranges, begging the question of how important it is if a new accountant or doctor is young and attractive.

Much of the sexism in Italian media originates in the television conglomerate owned by former prime minister Silvio Berlusconi. In 2010, I wrote a cover story for *Newsweek* magazine about Berlusconi's "women problem" (which I've touched on previously in this book) and how the party-girl portrayal of women as window dressing led to Italy's depressing ranking for equality in the World Economic Forum's Gender Gap report.[4]

I started the article with a description from a famous Italian television show called *Striscia la Notizia*, which remains both one of the smartest and stupidest programs on Berlusconi's network. Its format involves two male presenters who introduce hard-hitting stories, including interviews with criminals, serious takes on organized crime, and exposés on corruption across the country. But the men are always accompanied by two women—a blond and a brunette—whose only purpose is to titillate. The program does not need them, I argued. The story went viral and was picked up by the Italian press. I felt for a moment that I had started a conversation, maybe even one that would lead to change. It was a naive view.

In response to the article, while I was home one evening preparing dinner for my young sons, two uniformed police officers from Italy's elite Carabinieri military police knocked on my door to deliver a summons for criminal defamation against Berlusconi and the makers of the program. In my story, I had described how a very beautiful Black woman wearing a thong getup had slithered across the floor while one of the hosts held up a garlic strand attached to a belt that left little to the imagination in terms of its phallic reference. I had written that when she left the stage, one of the men had patted her bottom. I watched the footage over and over again and the way the woman jumped in surprise left no question in my mind that they had touched her derriere. But according to the lawsuit, the moment was scripted and there was no contact whatsoever—an alleged error that could have landed me in jail for three years since criminal defamation in Italy is a crime punishable by prison terms. *Newsweek* sent lawyers to defend me and the whole thing was settled out of court with the magazine running a rather comical letter by one of the show's producers about how they respect women. It was not so much a lesson as a warning to me that freedom of the press in this country, especially when it comes to the way women are treated, is completely dictated by "superior" men. The whole episode was as shocking as it was terrifying.

It was around that time that I met Monica through an organization that helps victims of extreme domestic violence, and since the rape was carried out by her own family members, she qualified. My intent was to try to showcase these stories of extreme sexual violence against women as another way to paint a picture not only of inequality in this country but also of impotence on the part of the country's structures to do anything to change it. What I learned through Monica was that the problem so often lies in women's own attitudes about themselves and their place on the social spectrum. "I was weak and thought I could just have an affair like my husband had before he went to jail," Monica told me. Shocking to me at the time, she had yet to decide if she would provide evidence against her family clan or just stay away for a while until she could "negotiate" a return, which I learned later is what she ultimately did.

If she had testified, she would have qualified to be entered into the Italian witness-protection program and given a new life. If she didn't testify, at some point she would have been released to fend for herself. What has come to make sense to me only after many years is that Monica just didn't believe that law enforcement could protect her or would be strong or even committed enough to stand up to the criminal group. I have no idea if she is still alive or what her sacrifice would have had to be to return to her family, but I have no reason to believe rape wasn't part of it.

I asked Pupetta if rape is common within the circles her father and Pasqualone were part of, and if they had ever been involved in doling out that sort of punishment. She told me that it happens only when it is "deserved." For example, if the daughter of an underboss betrays her mafioso boyfriend in a way that is publicly humiliating, it is "natural that some sort of punishment would be handed down." She said rape would ensure that no one else would date the woman, thereby inflicting a lifelong punishing for her mistake. "No one would ever want a woman who has been raped," Pupetta said in a way that made me realize she also agreed with the practice.

Rape is also used when mafia men are found out to be gay, which is unacceptable—in theory though not always in practice—across most of Italy's crime syndicates (again, the Neapolitan Camorra proving itself to be the most liberal of the three). It is even taboo to say the Italian word *omosessuale* (homosexual) around many of the criminal elders, as if canceling the word from the local dialect somehow means same-sex attraction doesn't exist at all.

A twenty-year-old gay man serving time for mafia-related crimes in 2007 in the Piazza Lanza prison in Catania, Sicily, was so brutally gang-raped by eight Cosa Nostra prisoners that he required multiple anal stitches. His lawyer, Antonio Fiumefreddo, told me in an interview that many of the bosses across the syndicates are gay but would never admit to it. "My client was honest, and he was punished for it," he said. "The rest live a double life until they get caught."

There are countless similar stories of terrifying and even deadly homophobia. One Camorra prisoner in the Santa Maria Capua Vetere prison in Naples was found hanged in the prison rec yard simply because an inmate in a cell next door thought he heard the man's Tunisian cellmate giving him a blow job. In Sicily, it's not just gay men who are shunned—if there is a gay person in an aspiring mafia member's family, the whole family cannot join the Cosa Nostra.[5] The same goes for any candidates whose parents are divorced.

Still, there are exceptions. In 2009, anti-mafia police in Naples swept in to arrest twenty-seven members of a powerful clan[6] tied to a growing drug and prostitution ring. The leader was Ugo "Kitty" Gabriele, the first known transgender mafia clan boss—or member for that matter—to be taken into custody in Italy. Kitty was ahead of her time, able to command the faction of her clan with total respect, which was doubly impressive given that she identified and dressed as a woman during a period when women were not always given credit as bosses. The arrest garnered transphobic sarcastic headlines in the local and international press undoubtedly because it was a full decade before global acceptance of transgender rights strived to put an end to such shaming.

Another case didn't end up with the same tolerance. Giovanna "Gió" Arrivoli was born female but identified as a male from a very young age. The forty-one-year-old aspiring Camorra clan boss had started undergoing gender-reassignment surgeries when he was tortured and fatally shot in 2016, reportedly after fellow clansmen learned he was trans. He was tortured for days and then killed with two shots to the heart and one in the brain and buried with only his head interred in the ground, which signified to police that it was a vengeance act for betrayal. His live-in girlfriend said he also had immense drug and gambling debts, which are rare among these criminals because they tend to be debt collectors rather than the ones taking on debt. But a police officer I asked about the crime told me he felt it was more likely he was killed for his gender identity.

It could also be that Gió's "deception" wasn't so much the problem as was the fact that his case angered many who are uninformed about gender issues, still shockingly common in Italy. The country has a poor record with trans rights in particular, and with the exception of a popular trans politician named Vladimir Luxuria, who never went through sex-reassignment surgery but whose insistence that she deserved to be respected as a woman despite being born male led to the Italian parliament installing a separate bathroom just for her. Lawmakers have since made it possible for people to change their names on legal documents, but changing one's gender remains a point of great debate and is decided on a case-by-case basis. It is also nearly impossible to list both names of same-sex parents on a birth certificate, or for same-sex couples to adopt children. Heterosexual couples can adopt stepchildren who are biologically connected to one of the parents, but gay couples still cannot. Even in cases of surrogacy or same-sex couples, only one parent can be named on the birth certificate.

Of course, for crime syndicates, there is one gray area: not all same-sex kisses are romantic. Few mafia observers will forget the startling image of twenty-seven-year-old Daniele D'Agnese, a key figure with one of the Camorra's most notorious clans, giving passionate full-on lip kisses to two younger male associates when they were arrested in Naples in 2011.[7] Many outsiders wondered what exactly it meant, but a key mafia analyst told me at the time that the kiss was a signal that the younger associates, who weren't yet bona fide clansmen, would not be left to defend themselves and, as such, ought not think about turning against the clan and cooperating with police.

"It was a sign to the weaker members of the group telling them, 'We'll continue to be a group; we'll command the same territory and whatever happens, you won't be abandoned,'" the analyst told me. Essentially, their oath was sealed with a kiss.

Less intimate kisses between the mafia's homophobic men have long held varying meanings. In Sicily, a kiss on the lips is a signal that the recipient is going to be killed. A kiss on the cheek in Naples is a sign of earned respect, and in Puglia, a kiss of the ring is a sign of submission in line with cardinals and bishops kissing the ring of a pope.

Some mafia dons to this day behave like men of God, spouting scripture and passing judgment by day and carrying out bloody raids or selling drugs that kill thousands of people at night. They pour money into church coffers, adhering to the strictest of Catholic commandments, with the apparent exceptions of "Thou shalt not steal," "Thou shalt not commit murder," and "Thou shalt not commit adultery." In exchange they are given God's blessing from the local priests who baptize their children, pray at their funerals, and forgive their sins.

I once interviewed a priest in truly godforsaken Castel Volturno, where the Camorra and Nigerian mafia engage in some of the worst criminality in all of Italy. The beach town was exploited by the Camorra-backed Coppola family in a post–World War II attempt to develop an Italian Miami Beach. The carcasses of apartment blocks confiscated and then abandoned by the state have become the stage for Nigerian sex trafficking and the heroin trade.

The priest, who volunteered at a center that tried to get the sex-trafficked Nigerian women off the streets, did his best to explain the complexities of the relationship between the Catholic Church in southern Italy and its various mafia groups, insisting that they both got from each other something no other entity could give: mafiosi can ask for blanket forgiveness for any manner of sins, and the church's coffers are often lined with blood money.

"It's a delicate balance," he said, admitting, "There is a lot of soul-searching to be done." The priest was arrested in late 2019 for aiding and abetting prostitution and later defrocked.

Things are changing, and the divide between the Catholic Church and the mafia has never been greater. Pope Francis was the first pontiff to address the problem outright, declaring in 2014 just after his election that all mafia members should be excommunicated from the Church, which made it difficult for local parish priests in mafia towns to continue to treat them as they did before. Decades earlier, Pope John Paul II had condemned the mafia, but never as strongly, instead likening silence against the mafia to complicity, but never going so far as to ban members from the Church. Francis decreed that the practice of stopping to pay homage in front of the homes of mafia dons during religious processions was also prohibited. The new rule, enacted in 2014, made it terribly uncomfortable for many small-town parish priests. They had for years counted on hefty donations in return for what looked like a blessing when parishioners, directed by the priests, would choreograph their annual saint processions to swing by important mafiosi homes to pay respects to their biggest donors.

Then at a ceremony in 2018 commemorating Father Giuseppe Puglisi, a priest who was shot at point-blank range on the front steps of a parsonage in Palermo in 1993 for refusing to perform baptisms, confessions, and even marriages for known mafiosi, Pope Francis said that you can't be in the mafia and believe in God. "A person who is a mafioso does not live as a Christian because with his life he blasphemes against the name of God," he said, complicating an already complicated relationship.

Pupetta's top-floor apartment was filled with religious iconography. Small saints were perched on nooks, and once when I visited her before Christmas she was putting the finishing touches on an elaborate nativity scene of the type Naples is so well-known for. I asked her if she went to Mass, and she crossed herself but didn't answer. She and Pasqualone were married in a massive Catholic wedding, and she still put flowers on his grave in the local Catholic cemetery until she died.

Pupetta's funeral was scheduled for New Year's Eve 2021 in the church of Sant'Antonio di Padova not far from her house. The flower wreaths with her name emblazoned on a ribbon adorned the church, and the traditional funeral announcement posters of her death and services were plastered on the metal billboards nearby with the date and time.

But the day before the funeral, the Questura of Naples—the local Neapolitan police authority—ruled that a public funeral could not be held, even dispatching police to make sure no one honored her or memorialized "Lady Camorra" in any way. Instead, the local parish priest blessed her coffin at the Castellammare di Stabia cemetery before it was slid into the family tomb. A group of women she had befriended traipsed from the church to the cemetery with the flowers meant for the altar to lay them near the tomb, but they, too, were turned away. Instead they went back to the church and prayed the rosary for her.

5

'Til Death Do Us Part

After her husband was murdered in 1976, she naturally supported her sons' bid to avenge their father's death—the killing was carried out by her thirteen-year-old, Antonio.

Pupetta's wedding scrapbook had a secret envelope hidden in a back flap where she kept a folded copy of her marriage license to Pasqualone. The typewritten document was faded and looked fake but for the marca di bollo stamp initialed by the court clerk. The date is two days before the lavish ceremony that brought five hundred friends and enemies to celebrate her Catholic wedding ceremony complete with high Mass.

Pupetta carefully unfolded the license and read it to me slowly, as if she had never seen it before. "We married for life," she said, not looking up. "I will never love anyone like that again."

Sometimes it seems as if Pupetta forgot that she was well into her eighties and that the prospect of falling in love again was remote. She loved Umberto when they first met, but she said that love died when he killed her son. "Sometimes I don't know why I stayed on so long," she said. "The twins needed a father, and I needed financial support, I guess. Women don't always make decisions based on the heart."

Sometimes mafia women instead ignore what should be common sense and really do blindly follow their hearts. Antonietta Bagarella, a once-slender, dark-eyed beauty, is a prime example of a woman who surely should have known what she was getting into when she married Cosa Nostra superboss Salvatore Totò Riina. His nicknames included la Belva, "the Beast," and Totò ú Curtu, "Totò the Short," which should have been a clue. But Antonietta married him anyway while he was a fugitive on the run for murder and used her devotion to her criminal husband as a cover that protected her from prosecution more than a few times. Ninetta, as she was locally known, was herself the daughter of a midlevel Cosa Nostra mobster who spent time in a high-security prison for mafia collusion but whose rank was far lower than one might assume to offer a daughter to such a high-ranking boss. She was the fifth of six children, and her mother was a hairdresser who ran a small business out of the family kitchen in Corleone. Ninetta was a teacher at the Sacred Heart College of Corleone in Sicily when she met the far less attractive don, who captured her heart despite the fact that he had committed his first homicide when he was just seventeen years old. Because Pupetta's husband died so early in their marriage it is impossible to know how their relationship would have played out, or if he, like Umberto, would have become a literal partner in crime. But Totò the Beast's influence over Ninetta was clear, and it undoubtedly kept her faithful over the years, given the unthinkable sacrifices she would have had to make—both emotionally and physically—to love such a bloodthirsty man and live so long in hiding.

Totò the Beast had a bird-beak mouth with thin lips and vacant eyes. Thick, tufted eyebrows made him look mean even on the rare occasions when he was not. That first homicide involved strangling a man with his bare hands as a rite of initiation ordered by his father to prove he was ready for the full Cosa Nostra membership.[1] Years later he was found responsible for the heinous deaths of anti-mafia judges Giovanni Falcone and Paolo Borsellino, and for the murder of a foe's young son, whom he dissolved in acid.

Soon after news of their romance got out, Ninetta lost her teaching job after the nuns she worked for asked police about her. The nuns, who already knew her father had served time for mafia affiliation, had seen her name mentioned in a local newspaper tied to the murderous criminal and had been too nervous to ask her personally about her rumored relationship. Instead they had gone to the authorities, who confirmed the nuns' worst fears. Confident they wouldn't face retaliation because of the long-held belief among many mafiosi that clergy are untouchable, they fired the teacher.

A year later, Ninetta was brought in by an anti-mafia magistrate, who accused her of running messages between various thugs hiding around Corleone. She faced a sentence of "internal exile"—which meant essentially sending her off to be alone somewhere in the country and strictly forbidding contact with anyone from home.

The use of such a punishment began in 1926 when Benito Mussolini ordered antifascists to remote islands and cutoff villages. It has been used periodically for mafia criminals, usually leading to the exilee's death from suicide sparked by extreme loneliness, paranoia, and fear. Ninetta escaped the unusual punishment entirely because she played the "weak woman" card, pretending to know nothing of her lover's line of work, even though she had lost her teaching job because of it. She was sent home, where she quietly slipped away to join her beloved mobster in hiding. Had she been convicted, she would have been the first woman to be sentenced to such exile.

Totò the Beast and Ninetta's relationship is somewhat of a fairy-tale love story, albeit one stained with blood. At the time, Totò was the most wanted fugitive in all of Italy. They married in a secret hideaway, but then famously spent their honeymoon gallivanting across Italy, spending the final days of their romantic getaway in Venice. That he was able to move so freely implied corruption in the police, who would have had to turn a blind eye. The complicity would have also extended to hotels, restaurants, and even the gondolier who took them through the romantic Venetian canals. Their faces were both recognizable from press reports, and not even a disguise would have kept them anonymous from all the people they would have encountered. Their marriage was spent moving between hideouts and in later years, prison visiting rooms. They raised four children in the twenty-four years they lived on the lam, during which time Totò was accused of ordering the deaths of 150 people. He was caught and jailed in 1993 and given multiple life sentences.

Totò the Beast died of kidney cancer in a maximum-security

prison in Sicily in 2017. Thanks to reforms that came into effect in the mid-1990s, big funerals are not allowed for mafia bosses, so Ninetta, having by then faded into a dowdy Sicilian nonna, had to lay him to rest at a private ceremony in the Corleone cemetery as photographers snapped photos through the wrought-iron gates. The cemetery priest, Father Giuseppe Gentile, gave an extended prayer and blessed the coffin before it was interred, but he could not conduct a full funeral—at least not in public. More than a few journalists reported that Father Gentile had, in fact, secretly conducted the Catholic funeral rite before Totò the Beast was hauled to the graveyard after the family made a sizeable donation to his church coffers.

The Beast was buried in the family tomb, which is adorned by a statue of the venerated Padre Pio and permanent flower vases that Ninetta still fills with fresh chrysanthemums every week. Three of the couple's children, Maria Concetta, Lucia, and Giuseppe Salvatore, attended the funeral, indignantly batting away the press from behind dark glasses of the kind one might envision on a celebrity as they arrived and left. (Their fourth child, Giovanni, was already serving a life sentence for a quadruple homicide at the time.)

When Totò the Beast was locked in a high-security prison, the job of running the Corleonesi clan of the Sicilian mafia fell on Bernardo "Binnu u tratturi" (the Tractor) Provenzano, whose nicknames also included il ragioniere (the accountant). He was already living in hiding when he came into power after being sentenced to life in the so-called Maxi Trial of the 1980s, which was fed by the confessions of turncoat Tommaso Buscetta, an associate of Pupetta's Umberto.

Provenzano was never married but was romantically linked to Saveria Palazzollo, herself tied to a criminal family, thus completing the circle. She was a tall, striking woman who was considerably younger than the Tractor, and the two spent their entire relationship in hiding, where they nonetheless had two children.

Before anyone linked her to Provenzano, she was investigated for a slew of her own property and business purchases made over a period of just five months in the early 1970s. Her acquisitions included a construction company, land near Pupetta's hometown of Castellammare, and a lavish apartment in Palermo. The transactions drew suspicion because Palazzollo had no tax record of income and because her accountant was a known money launderer for the Cosa Nostra. But when police searched for her, they soon learned she was on the lam with Provenzano. A few months after they were on her trail, she sold the properties to a mafia-related company through her shady accountant without ever surfacing, though the forms to finalize the sales—mostly in cash—were all signed by her.

Saveria was tried for money laundering in absentia in 1990. But she did send in her excuse: in a letter to the magistrate, she explained that her windfall came from an elderly aunt and she was essentially trying to obtain her own financial independence and unknowingly consulted the wrong advisers, whom she blamed for the dealings that led to her charges. She was eventually sentenced in absentia to house arrest, but because she was in hiding, the sentence was never enforced. When she eventually surfaced, the statute of limitations had run out.

Meanwhile, with Totò kept in isolation in prison, prohibiting even Ninetta from visiting for years, Bernardo the Tractor pressed ahead with the drug smuggling, extortion, and murder Totò had intended for the organization. Bernardo cut a boxy figure, and his youthful pompadour made his earliest mug shots look almost like model-agency headshots; his last mug shot after years in hiding made him look like a bloated Elvis. He got his nickname the Tractor not for his size, but because he liked to "mow people down."[2]

In 1992, after the twin assassinations of anti-mafia magistrates Falcone and Borsellino at the hands of Saveria and Ninetta's men—crimes that inspired Alessandra Cerreti to become an anti-mafia prosecutor—the women showed up together suddenly in Corleone, returning home seemingly out of thin air in a taxi one day after being in hiding for more than a decade. They had with them their six secret children—the two that Saveria had with the Tractor, and the four Ninetta had with the Beast, all born in hiding and without birth certificates or documents of any sort.

The presence of the women at such a volatile time confirmed to many that their husbands knew they would soon be arrested or killed, and they wanted to give their women and children an opportunity to find relative safety. Neither wife cooperated with police, and both swore they had no idea where their husbands were, despite the relatively young ages of the kids, who were not DNA tested.

Ninetta and Saveria are quintessential old-style mafia women, both investigated for crimes relating to their husbands' work time and again, but never taken seriously as leaders in their own right, in part because their partners were the capo dei capi, or boss of bosses—it is unlikely these women would ever have been able to fill their partners' shoes. But sheltered as they were by law enforcement's prejudice, both women could have been far more involved in every aspect of their husbands' work, not just delivering messages or hiding secrets, but acting as true confidantes.

When Bernardo the Tractor was captured in 2006 after forty-three years on the run, he was living in a ramshackle farmhouse near Corleone, where investigators found ninety religious statues, five Bibles, and a well-used rosary hanging next to the toilet. On the table beside his bed was an unfinished letter to his striking blond wife. The love letter was still on the roller of the Olivetti typewriter he used to compose the secret messages that were delivered to the mafia soldiers across the island and beyond. He was accused of ordering the deaths of at least four hundred people.

A year before he was caught, Bernardo the Tractor had apparently moved to a new hideout closer to Corleone, which is a town of just over eleven thousand people, making its per capita mafia membership one of the highest in Italy. He wanted to be closer to Saveria, though the two had not seen each other in the months before his capture as a precaution to make sure she wouldn't be trailed. But he hadn't put enough distance between him and the wife he was trying to protect. She couldn't stop herself from preparing him fresh pasta and making sure he had clean, ironed laundry. Police say they caught him by trailing a trusted delivery man who had the task of taking the ironed shirts and underwear from Saveria's house in town to her husband in the hinterland.

They pounced when he opened the farmhouse door to bring Saveria's parcel inside.

"Women have always unwittingly been the ruin of criminals on the run," Nicola Cavaliere, the anti-mafia investigator in charge of the operation, said when announcing the capture. "So it was in Provenzano's case that a woman committed a fatal error that led to his capture."

Blaming Saveria, who at forty-eight was far younger than the seventy-four-year-old Tractor, deserves scrutiny. Police found thousands of secret messages, called pizzini, rolled into tiny parcels and taped tight, ready to be sent out along with intricate codes with the apparently sacred key written into the Bibles he kept at the farm. Investigators had seen these pizzini before, and they knew they came directly from Bernardo. With all the movement of the messages in and out of that little shack, it seems impossible that it was Saveria's laundry that finally cracked the case. More likely, police were trailing him for many months and waiting until the perfect moment to nab him. A Sicilian anti-mafia detective who wouldn't consent to being named told me during an interview in Palermo that it was easier to blame Saveria's "silly housewife mistake" for his capture. "Blaming a pizzini courier or even a foot soldier would have tipped off the whole network they were onto them," he said, implying that the general population wouldn't question the explanation that a housewife's mistake had cost the capo dei capi his freedom.

Among the many notes police decoded from the handwritten legend scrawled inside one of the Bibles were several to his doctor asking for treatments for impotence. Bernardo had been smuggled to Nice, France, a few years earlier for prostate surgery and suspected cancer, and had apparently had a difficult time with erectile dysfunction after that. He was clearly preparing for the moment Saveria could visit, and the doctor had prescribed and arranged for delivery of Viagra among other, herbal remedies.

With the Tractor now in prison, *La Repubblica* newspaper interviewed Saveria, who insisted they had it "all wrong" about her beloved Bernardo[3] and that he wasn't the brutal killer they made him out to be. She told the reporters she planned to live out her days in her quiet hometown. "Normally, Corleone is a peaceful country," she told the paper. "Nothing serious ever happens and nothing particularly important happens here."

Provenzano died from bladder cancer in a Milan maximum-security prison in 2016. He was cremated and his ashes interred in the same cemetery as his former associate Totò the Beast, just a few rows away. Provenzano, too, was denied any final send-off that would have allowed his foot soldiers to mourn him, and the family ultimately decided to have him cremated in Milan and place his urn in the family mausoleum, though Saveria was able to secure a priest for a private ceremony.

As criminal organizations have evolved across Italy, the significant roles played by women like Ninetta and Saveria, who did not assume leadership but also never left the side of the vicious bosses they married, have not so much evolved as they have been reconsidered. Saveria, especially, has skimmed along the edges of legality for years. Her name showed up on a number of properties owned by her late husband's associates that were only recently confiscated in a search for the current boss of bosses, Matteo Messina Denaro. She lives freely in Corleone, despite having been on the lam with one of the biggest bosses in the history of the Sicilian Cosa Nostra. One of her sons now gives mafia tours in Palermo, pointing out to curious tourists various spots where murders and heists took place.

Ninetta has fallen silent since the death of her husband, though all of her assets—around $1.5 million worth—were seized in 2019, tied to her son-in-law's alleged mafia affiliation. One of the Riina daughters, born while they were hiding out, married into a mob family, undoubtedly blessed not only by her father but by Ninetta.

"Women have long been invisible in Italian mafias," Rossella Selmini, a professor of criminology and sociology at universities in Bologna and Minneapolis, wrote in a 2020 paper published by the University of Chicago. Like Mafia analyst Ernesto Savona, who argued that the rise of women in mafia ranks is a result of "sweet criminal organizations," Selmini goes on to say that stronger law-enforcement tactics and tougher laws have forced the various organized-crime syndicates to "become more professional, smaller, more flexible, and less violence-based" and that means "the roles of women became more important." Not only does that ignore the number of women who have blood on their hands and who are in prison for their crimes, Selmini concedes that the increased role of women also could be just a change in perception. Law enforcement is finally considering women as capable criminals rather than hapless arm candy.

Both Provenzano's and Riina's partners were questioned

multiple times about what they knew, then always let go despite being the two people closest to the most wanted men in the country. Both live freely even today. But both lived with their mafia men on the run for decades, most of the time presumably alone, which begs several questions about life on the lam and whether they were protected and hidden. Neither have ever spoken publicly or to investigators about the dynamics, especially about the education of their children who spoke perfect German.

Gaetano Guida, a notable pentito against the Camorra, was the first to really pull back the curtain on women's roles in the Neapolitan syndicate. While delivering information in exchange for his freedom from prosecution and a new identity, he told investigators that women were "on the front line" of the organization's criminal activity. He gave crucial testimony against Maria Licciardi, known as La Piccolina and La Principessa, or the little one and the princess, the younger sister of a notable Camorra crime boss. At a distance, her closely cropped hairstyle made her at times indistinguishable from a man, especially in grainy surveillance footage. You might think, too, that her considerable crimes made her indistinguishable from a man, until you get close enough to realize that, as early as Pupetta, women have been playing far less subtle roles in mafia activity and vendettas than the stories of Ninetta and Saveria suggest. Maria, who is now in her sixties, famously avenged the murder of her nephew by ordering the deaths of fourteen rivals in a span of just forty-eight hours in the late 1980s, a veritable slaughter in contrast to Pupetta's first murder. She also sent out lists of people who were on *her* death row, even reportedly post-ing death notices of rivals she intended to kill to warn them they were next.

She escaped capture many times, including once when police homed in on her hideout in a dilapidated farmhouse that was actually a lavish villa inside, complete with a grand piano, mar-ble floors, and a hot tub. She was finally arrested in 2001 as she tried to escape town while hiding on the floor of the back seat of a car with a newly married couple still wearing their wedding best. She served eight years in prison, from where she still com-manded the family. She also famously ordered the clans under her watch to not sell pure unfiltered heroin that came from Is-tanbul, Turkey, out of fear it was too strong and would kill off the clan's client base. One of the groups under her watch defied her orders, chafing against a woman at the helm, and sold the heroin anyway, which killed dozens of addicts across Naples in a short period of time. Her punishment for those who betrayed her authority was making them use the drug, killing several clansmen, according to a turncoat who testified against her. The deaths were made to look like accidental overdoses, but in at least one case, Licciardi is said to have personally overseen what amounted to a forced overdose.

She was released from prison in 2009. An arrest warrant was once again issued for her in June 2019, but it was rescinded a month later and she remained a free woman despite her docu-mented criminal past and rather impressive death toll. She was finally arrested on a new arrest warrant while trying to board a flight to Spain from Rome's smaller Ciampino Airport as part of a sting operation tied to a massive raid on the Secondigliano Alliance. She was charged with running an extortion racket near Naples and, as of this writing, awaits trial.

"On more than one occasion, she transmitted her older brothers' orders to kill," Guida the pentito said about La Principessa. "The women took on all sorts of jobs on behalf of the alliance: They took messages to prisoners, distributed money to members, organized activities, especially numbers running and extortion rackets. In other words, they constitute the backbone of the organization."[4]

Maria Campagna, a Cosa Nostra lady boss whom one turncoat called "a woman with balls,"[5] is a case in point of underestimation. Investigators initially thought Maria took over the reins after her husband, Salvatore "Turi" Cappello's drug network that spanned from Calabria to Sicily to Naples landed him a life sentence in jail. But after a deeper investigation in 2017, dubbed Operation Penelope, sent thirty people to prison, it was clear that Maria and her husband were equal partners in the lucrative enterprise they launched as a team in 2012. Together they took the lives of around 150 people. Zia Maria (Aunt Maria), as she was often called, narrowly escaped conviction around the time the two were launching their criminal endeavor. Even then, well into the 2000s, police underestimated her criminal intent and let her go—which emboldened her to reach even greater heights in the criminal world and ultimately kill even more people.

Zia Maria was a flat-faced woman who wore her hair back like a schoolmarm and was almost always without makeup because her husband was almost always in jail. She moved from

Catania in Sicily to her hometown of Naples, where she ran the I Due Vulcani (Two Volcanoes) pizzeria named for Etna in Sicily and Vesuvius over Naples. The ramshackle restaurant, which is now operated under new management, was not far from the train station and provided a perfect cover for Zia Maria's criminal enterprise.

Initially, investigators assumed she had moved back home to Naples with her son to get away from the illegality. But in actuality, Sicilian foot soldiers under her control would travel to Naples to receive their marching orders. Basic instructions from Salvatore were hidden in elaborate doctored photos that he made on a prison computer and printer—instructions that she then made more specific. (Salvatore had gained access to the computer equipment while pursuing a sudden interest in obtaining a degree in graphic design. Zia Maria took the products of this "schoolwork" with her and mailed them out as greeting cards and thank-you notes.) Since she was on the outside, only she had the direct knowledge about what was really happening on the streets, how much money was being made and lost, and who needed to be killed or threatened. She and Salvatore could not speak about criminal activity in prison, since all of their conversations—as with many Italian prisoners—were being surveilled. So it was ultimately up to her to interpret what Salvatore wanted, and ultimately to determine whether her husband's instructions were the right course of action to follow.

Zia Maria represents a growing number of women who have the controlling majority in mafia-run businesses. In her case, it was not just on paper, as is often believed. The Italian research center Transcrime found in a 2019 study that while only

2.5 percent of those who go to prison for mafia crimes are women, they are listed as sole owners of more than one third of all confiscated mafia assets. That's twice as many women shareholders than in all of Italy's legal economy, according to the group.[6]

Ample evidence points to the fact that wives have always played a greater role than just providing cover. When Pupetta's husband was shot in broad daylight, he was immediately surrounded by associates who wanted to know who pulled the trigger. Those men ran when the police arrived, but Pasqualone would tell only Pupetta who his assassin was, which both transferred the responsibility of the vendetta to her and showed his collaborators that he trusted no one more than her. Based on their intimate complicity, it's hard to imagine the sort of criminal enterprise Pupetta and Pasqualone could have achieved had he survived.

Anna Mazza, the "black widow" of Camorra kingpin Gennaro Moccia, whose territory extended to the city limits of Naples, evolved into one of the bloodiest and most powerful female bosses of her era. After her husband was murdered in 1976, she naturally supported her sons' bid to avenge their father's death[7]—it was eventually carried out by her thirteen-year-old son, Antonio. But then she went beyond just supporting her son's vengeful foray. She also directed the clan's bloodiest operations and was eventually convicted of mafia collusion—the first woman in Italy to be sentenced for such a crime—for which she served a mere five years in prison.

She groomed her sons in the image of their criminal father, and they made her proud. She managed the political relationships that are an integral part of the Camorra's infiltration of government and legitimate enterprise, and she was relatively unhindered until her late seventies. A squat woman with a round face frequently hidden behind a signature pair of Jackie O sunglasses, she made her rounds with a fully armed female security detail. In the 1980s, she pretended to disassociate herself from the Camorra in a bid to spring one of her sons from jail. She died in her eighties in 2017 and her lavish funeral was attended by about a hundred guests in the Catholic church of Sant'Antonio ad Afragola outside Naples. Pupetta attended her funeral and called Anna a "family friend."

Another woman who went beyond what was expected is Paola Altamura, who was born into a highly regarded criminal family in Taranto, Puglia, a dirty town that sits at the insole of Italy's boot. Puglia's Sacra Corona Unita mafia is mostly dead by now, but factions of it sprout up from time to time. Taranto is known best for toxic pollution from the ArcelorMittal steel factory known as ex-Ilva, which has led to childhood cancer rates 21 percent higher than anywhere else in the region (though still lower than on the slopes of Mount Vesuvius, where the Camorra plants toxic waste on the shin of Italy's boot). The entire town wakes up each morning blanketed in a thin layer of toxic rust that floats down from the factory, but no one wants to close it because it employs so many people.

In a court case that landed Paola and seventy others in jail for mafia collusion, the streaky-haired blonde was described as a "determined, bloodthirsty woman" who was actively involved in the crimes—including murder—committed by her sixteen children who formed the Apesso clan. The group dealt mostly in drug and arms trafficking across the Adriatic Sea and beyond, and they dabbled in racketeering and extortion for good measure. The judge in the case determined that the matriarch Paola was the mastermind behind the arms-distribution wing of the clan, the one who decided who needed what weaponry depending on the job to be done. She was also involved in the packaging of the myriad drugs sold by the clan (and was notoriously frugal in her measurements).

But the most notorious of the mafia wives is easily Anna Addolorata De Matteis Cataldo, or, as her associates called her, Anna Morte, "Anna Death." Born in Puglia in the ornate town of Lecce, often referred to as the Florence of the South, Anna Death and her husband were sentenced to life in prison for ordering the death of a rival by firing squad using Kalashnikovs. The court described their actions as driven by "despicable motives connected to conflicts for supremacy in the criminal underworld."[8] She also devised a plan to rig up the door of a shopkeeper who refused to pay protection money, keeping him under constant threat that she could blow up the place with him inside at any time if he didn't let her associates take goods without paying.

But it was her subsequent life sentence for the murder of Paola Rizzello and her two-year-old daughter for which she will be most remembered. Mrs. Rizzello apparently had secret information about Anna Death's husband—at first as his secret lover and later as a witness to a murder he allegedly carried out. Anna Death could not risk the other woman going to the police, so she ordered a heinous hit, burning Mrs. Rizzello's body and throwing it down a cistern. She also buried her baby daughter Angelica's body nearby. The infant's remains were found nearly eight years later. Anna Death's husband, by then also incarcerated, was apparently appalled at his wife's unbounded cruelty.

Pupetta was visibly shaken at the mention of the violence with which her successors in the underworld operate. She told me that while the murder she committed was hardly clean, it was "with good intention." She wondered how women could order the killing of children. "It's a step too far. There is justification under certain circumstances to seek revenge," she said. "But there is never justification to kill a child. Never." As she said this, I couldn't help wondering if she was talking about the death of her first son and the man she continued to live with after the boy's disappearance.

Sometimes Pupetta's claims of moral high ground betray her. I could never help thinking that under the right circumstances, she, too, could transgress to a degree that would horrify even the male bosses in her criminal world. A heavily pregnant woman who can murder someone in cold blood has a certain edge of calm. While she was ultimately acquitted for the murder of Semerari, she was certainly capable of it and, at least for one set of judges who heard her case, guilty. But her criminal acumen goes far beyond violence. Pupetta remained incredibly skilled at manipulation, right up until her death.

In 1982, she summoned the press to a press conference that many thought might be about the missing Pasqualino. Instead she stood at the podium, a leopard print scarf around the collar of her tight dress, and made a death threat to her foe Raffaele

Cutolo. "You know you have to leave me and mine alone, and you know that if you don't, I will be able to exterminate your whole family," she said, adding, "including the babies in the cribs."

Her subtle manipulation was even more frightening. She was in complete control at all times, even when she was feigning weakness. She was masterfully dishonest. But it was in those moments when I felt Pupetta was being brutally honest with me, only to find out later she was lying about everything she said, that I both admired and feared her the most.

6

Toxic Parents

Police refused to let her attend her murdered toddler's funeral, out of fear it could spark a gangland war if she showed up.

Pupetta's surviving children never had a dependable father figure. But Pupetta's relationship with her own father was formative. He was caught up in the trade of contraband cigarettes, and Pupetta remembered hiding his stolen goods in her dollhouse. He was not a top-tier crime boss, but he was well respected among the ranks of the Camorra. "I loved Papa dearly," she said. "He was such a role model to us all. He taught us so much about what is important and how to read people."

In Italy, the father-daughter relationship is a special one, with many fathers treating their daughters like princesses and fiercely protecting them from what they consider to be unqualified suitors. Like so many other facets of organized crime, the familial structures that exist in the larger Italian society provide the context for mafia families, too. It is no secret that Italian society also tends to embrace the mother-son relationship, with an abundance of thirty-year-old "mammoni" who don't leave Mamma's home until they can move straight into their wife's, so they'll never have to actually cook for themselves or do their own laundry. This holds especially true in mafia families.

Roberto, Pupetta's son with Umberto, is a case in point. He had odd jobs, mostly thanks to family friends, and even owned a car dealership in Rome. But he had trouble keeping steady work, undoubtedly because of his family baggage. When Mom has been convicted for murder no less than twice and Dad's a pentito, it is hard to get anyone to give you the keys to anything.

Pupetta's only daughter, Antonella, was more of a confidante to her mother, at times living in her house and taking her to doctor's appointments or bringing in groceries, and certainly protecting her in her old age, though it is hard to say exactly from what. Antonella wanted to monetize her mother's notoriety. She would sell her mother's interviews and tried desperately to stop her mother from talking to anyone unless there was a transaction of some sort.

Loyalty among daughters in mafia groups is often as unbreakable as it is easily manipulated. Jole Figliomeni, the daughter of the powerful Figliomeni crime family, with its tentacles extending from Calabria to Canada, is one of the best examples of how far a daughter will go to please her father.

Jole is a strong blond force to be reckoned with. Her social-media profile—when it was still available—was a bulletin board of glamour shots and selfies, often showing her on the arm of men in dark sunglasses or sitting on very nice cars. She has an international sense of style, mostly garnered from visiting family in the northern suburbs of Toronto, where she told me she spent at least some of her high school years, though finding a record of attendance at her supposed alma mater has proven impossible. She is multilingual, speaking English, French, and some Arabic, as well as Italian—rare for a girl from the unremarkable seaside town of Siderno, which hugs the arch of Italy's boot and where her father, Alessandro, was a mob-tied mayor for many years.

Her dad was arrested and pegged as a top 'Ndrangheta boss in 2010, which coincided with Siderno being named as the capital of the 'Ndrangheta's narco empire. Before his arrest and the total collapse of the local Figliomeni network, Jole hooked up with a married man whose jilted wife was the sister of a rival clan boss who outranked her own family. The sultry affair was reported in the society pages of the local paper as if the families were legitimate celebrities, and it nearly caused a clan civil war—and Jole's death.[1] Her father's arrest and the revelation that indeed he was one of the 'Ndrangheta's most important bosses in his own right watered down the scandal of the illicit affair because it put Jole on a more even playing field with the scorned wife.

But around 2015, it was all too much, and Jole suddenly decided to leave town, feigning disgust with her father, the 'Ndrangheta, and her former lover. She moved to Ivory Coast to start over. By not-so-odd coincidence, the African nation was conveniently emerging as one of the 'Ndrangheta's most important cocaine-trafficking hubs.

That's when I first reached out to Jole via Twitter, which she no longer uses—or at least not under her real name. It seems unfathomable that someone seemingly so needy of anonymous approval as she was when she first went to Africa would be able to go entirely incognito. At the time, I was researching female turncoats, which I thought she was, and which I was sure would be the focus of this book until I realized that the bad girls were much more interesting than the good ones. She was cordial and brief, answering my questions via Twitter's messaging platform in short missives peppered with requests to follow, retweet, or promote her in any way I could.

"No, I do not know anyone from Calabria here in the Abidjan," she once wrote.

"Yes, it's a coincidence that the 'Ndrangheta is here as well," she agreed.

And, "Sure, I guess it's harder to escape than you think."

We messaged about Canada and her family and my own family there, whether either of us could see ourselves living with such cold winters after the heat of Italy. But mostly she wanted to talk about the consultancy business she said she was trying to set up in the publishing industry. Time and again, she asked for contacts and help in getting her new project off the ground, which is generally a red flag for me during an interview because it shows that the source is not as well-placed as I had originally thought. This wasn't necessarily the case with Jole, though. Instead, she had an impressive social-media following in Ivory Coast—much more than she had in Italy. I later determined that she was actually trying to recast her persona outside of Italy, so if anyone tried to verify who she was they wouldn't come across her family's mob ties first.

During her first year or so in Ivory Coast, Jole spent her time between the busy port of Abidjan and the smaller inland town of Doropo on the border with Ghana and Burkina Faso. A newspaper article in her hometown Calabria paper *La Riviera* even ran an interview with her in October 2013. She sent me the clip. In it, she was described as "a manager in a cybersecurity firm in Abidjan" and the article focused on her efforts to make Siderno and Doropo "sister cities."

The Organized Crime and Corruption Reporting Project also reached her around that same time, and she told them in an email that she felt she needed to move to a developing nation "to be valued" for her abilities and "not to be pre-judged based on personal things that happened to my father."[2]

Meanwhile, back in Calabria, authorities were closing in on an investigation tying Jole to the 'Ndrangheta's dealings that utilized Abidjan and Antwerp, Belgium. The Calabrian criminal group had started to shuttle cocaine and heroin from South America through Abidjan to avoid shipping it directly to Europe, which had proven risky. Antwerp was at the time emerging as the port of choice for Europe's cocaine and heroin traffickers. Port workers were easily bribed to turn a blind eye to cargo containers from South America, from where drugs had for years been shipped.

Through wiretaps released in 2014, it became clear that anti-mafia investigators had an inkling that Jole did not leave the 'Ndrangheta behind after all and was certainly no pentita. She had apparently acted as a fixer of sorts for 'Ndrangheta agents looking to set up contacts in Ivory Coast, which she did at the request of her father, who she very likely had known all along was a drug baron. In one police transcript, a local drug lord is heard telling another man how thankful he was for Jole's help in Ivory Coast. "If it wasn't for her, we would be ruined," he said. "I don't understand the language. I know nothing. Fuck. Well, I mean I came here precisely to see her."

The lengthy investigation and wiretaps also turned up that the larger criminal population had a lurid interest in Jole's disastrous love life. Even in Canada, thugs who remembered her when she visited as a teenager were caught up in the Kardashi-anesque soap-opera details of her affair, discussing who was more at fault: the mob-mayor's daughter they knew from way back or the philandering boss? In the end, it was decided—and thus speculated in the tabloid press—that Jole's married lover broke the code of ethics for disrespecting his wife. That the wiretaps were peppered with such banal observations at first led investigators to believe perhaps Jole's love life was a cover for something else, or that by mentioning the affair mobsters were really talking about drug deals or murder hits. In fact, they were just gossiping.

Those wiretaps led to the arrest of twenty-three people tied to the Figliomeni clan, including several in the Toronto suburb of York. Five years later, in 2019, the same joint-op forces with the reinforcement of more than five hundred officers set out to arrest twenty-eight people in both York and Siderno. Canadian authorities seized millions in assets in raids that lasted seventy-two hours. The cache included $1 million in cash and another $1 million in gaudy jewelry, forty-eight restaurants and cafés, twenty-seven luxury homes, and twenty-three luxury cars, including five high-spec Ferraris. One Ferrari alone had a value of $672,000. They also found ATMs, video lottery terminals, and several exotic animals.

There is still some speculation that Jole's early intentions in getting out of Italy were genuinely to escape her family's influence, but that she was quickly sucked back into the only life she knew, either by force or choice. The truth may never be known. She has never cooperated with police, despite countless opportunities to turn. But it remains a curiosity why she would choose Ivory Coast—where the 'Ndrangheta was setting up contacts—when there were plenty of other developing countries she could have moved to had she really wanted a fresh start. More likely, her story was a ruse. A woman running off over a broken heart remains the perfect cover under which to build her daddy's business from the ground up—and a believable one in a country like Italy, where women are so often portrayed as weak, hysterical, and driven by emotion. She has never been arrested, and at present, has not been heard from again.

Jole's loyalty to her father is hardly unique among mafia spawn. Totò the Beast had two daughters who remain dedicated to their family history and seem to hover in the shady area of Italy's not-yet-convicted set.

In the summer of 2019, just two years after she helped bury her felonious father, the Beast's youngest daughter, Lucia, moved to Paris to "reinvent herself" after being refused a state-funded "baby bonus" that all new parents in Italy were receiving at the time to help counter the negative national birth rate.

She was told that the state could not reward her for having a child because of her father's sordid reputation, even though she had never been investigated for any crimes herself. That she was neither a pentita nor apologetic for Dad's reign of blood-stained terror helped little. Neither did the fact that in Paris she could have lived anonymously but chose to exploit her family name. She sold her abstract art on a website called Lucia Riina Art, where she peddled countless depictions of pale women with orange eyeliner and pouty lips painted on slabs of wood or canvas as well as blotchy landscapes clearly labeled as her home-town, Corleone, where the deadliest Riina of all had long ruled in infamy. Such a reputation might have caused some daughters to shy away from the use of the name, but she seemed to revel in it, or at least she learned how to successfully exploit it.

Lucia and her husband acquired a license to open a sleek Ital-ian restaurant they decorated with brown shutters and darkened windows just a few blocks from the Champs-Élysées in the fashionably expensive 8th arrondissement. She called the estab-lishment, which advertises authentic Sicilian food, Corleone by Lucia Riina.

Inside, on the paneled walls, hang photos of her infamous dad and the Riina family crest adorned with a lion holding a human heart. Using the name Corleone, an obvious mob refer-ence outside of Italy thanks to *The Godfather* enterprise, drew scorn from the families of the many hundreds of victims of Lucia's father's bloody tenure as the boss of bosses.

It also angered Nicolò Nicolosi, the mayor of Corleone, who complained to me in an interview that his fight to distance his city's name from mafia crime was not helped by the daughter of the city's biggest criminal so brazenly exploiting it. "How do we disassociate ourselves from a scourge like this?" he asked. "A restaurant with our town name associated with Totò Riina will damage our reputation." Nicolosi's predecessor in city hall, it must be noted, loved Francis Ford Coppola's treatment of Mario Puzo's trilogy and the Hollywood fairy dust that lifted the dusty hilltop town to global infamy as mafia aficionados flocked to the city.

In fact, before the pandemic, thousands of tourists each year would visit Corleone's mafia museum, which showcases bullets used in real hits and newspaper clippings and media images about real crimes. More recently, guided walking tours have been on offer that take mafia aficionados to spots where hits were carried out. Provenzano's former hideaway, which is now called Laboratorio della Legalita (Legal Laboratory), has walls covered with artistic renditions—often in abstract form—of paintings of mafia massacres spanning a period from 1943 to 1997 and is a highlight of the tours.

Nevertheless, despite the ensuing scandal surrounding the Corleone restaurant in Paris, the high-end eatery has consistently positive TripAdvisor ratings from people who, whether they admire or despise the subtle references, always seem to love the authentic Italian cuisine. Lucia, it must be said, does not personally run the restaurant; she delegates that task to minions and instead spends her time between Paris, Geneva, and Corleone.

Totò the Beast's older daughter, Maria Concetta Riina, took capitalizing on her grandfather one step further. Together with her husband, Antonino Ciavarello, she opened an online store in 2017 called Zu Totò, which in local dialect translates to Uncle Toto. The idea was to cash in on the Beast's notorious reputation with "Zu Totò branded products," such as coffee pods and keychains. The intent of turning a fast buck, the couple said, was to raise the capital needed to expand the company's inventory because, as the website explained, "they," meaning the state, "confiscated everything for no reason."

The site goes on to reference the Riina family coat of arms and, apparently, all that it stands for. "Thanks in advance for your trust," a post on the site says. "The lion is wounded but not dead. He will soon rise and continue to fight as he always has. Always."

Activity on the Zu Totò website was frozen in 2019 after Maria Concetta was placed under investigation for dealings tied to a London company called Formations House, which billed itself as an agency that "helped develop and manage new companies." The company website bragged that it had created "over 400,000 companies, partnerships, and trusts" and sold 25,000 "ready-made companies and partnerships" through twelve financial jurisdictions.[3]

British authorities had a different take on Formations House, alleging it was a cover for seasoned and wannabe criminals to anonymously launder money and conceal taxes. The company has been investigated countless times yet has remained unscathed, thanks to a number of loopholes that may now close post-Brexit. The whole business was run by an elderly woman named Edwina Coales, who, it turned out, had been dead for quite some time yet somehow managed to stay listed as CEO of more than a thousand of the dodgy enterprises, even signing off on all the transactions, apparently from the grave. As of publication, the company was somehow still running, albeit under the watchful eye of British authorities, who demanded that the dead grandmother's name be removed from the books.

Maria Concetta had dealings with the company as far back as 2007, when it opened a business for her called T&T Corp. Ltd. The company was registered to her, her husband, and Katia La Placa, the daughter of another Cosa Nostra boss from Corleone. T&T Corp. descriptions say it dealt with the import and export of wine, oil, and coffee, but what caught the eye of Italian authorities was its advertisement for "40-day lightning-quick divorces" in Italy, where the average divorce takes more than a decade, thanks to the influence of the Catholic Church. T&T Corp. was eventually given a citation for offering divorce papers without anyone on the payroll possessing a valid license to practice law. But the owners' real loss came in 2019, when the Italian state confiscated $1.7 million in profits the Beast's daughter had saved up—thanks to a law that allows the sequester of assets from heirs of non-pentito mafiosi.

Not all children of mafia dons grow up to enrich themselves on their father's terrible legacy. It used to be said that the mafia didn't touch children, but that rule is being ignored with greater frequency—the aforementioned Anna Death might have been just the beginning. In 2018, Francesca Castellese, the Sicilian mother of a dead teen named Giuseppe di Matteo, was awarded more than $2 million by the state in damages for her son's death under regulations that award victims of mafia crimes damages, despite the fact that she waited twenty-one full days after her son disappeared to report him missing.

Giuseppe's father, Santino, was a Cosa Nostra underboss who had turned state's evidence against the Sicilian mafia, a betrayal for which the boy's death was an inevitable act of revenge.

The thirteen-year-old was kidnapped in 1993 from a horse barn where he was preparing to ride his favorite horse. The men who grabbed him were disguised as anti-mafia police who had promised that he could see his father in protective custody. The boy is said to have told them he wanted to join his father. Instead, they tortured him for 779 days to try to get Santino to withdraw his testimony about the gory details of the murder of anti-mafia judge Giovanni Falcone. Photos of the boy in various stages of torture were also sent to his grandfather, also a Cosa Nostra member who, along with Francesca, tried in vain to convince Santino to change his mind.

Santino refused, and Giuseppe was slowly strangled to death on his fifteenth birthday, according to another pentito who was there—and who later described the boy's anguished cries for his father as he gasped his last breath.

The pentito said Giuseppe's body was dissolved in acid. The death was recognized by the state as a mafia crime, even though many of his own family members had never left the criminal world. As such, Santino's death was considered by the public to have been an internal affair. Outrage ensued that the state's fund for victims of mafia crimes was used to pay Castellese, who had, after all, tried to convince her husband to retract his testimony and stay in the syndicate and only repented years later telling investigators that, despite being married to a top mafioso for fifteen years, she was shocked to find out that he was in the Cosa Nostra. As a pentita, she was required to testify in several trials, but each time she broke down in uncontrollable tears, rendering her testimony useless. Magistrates and prosecutors pleaded with the court to not make her suffer through the details of her son's terrible death, but in doing so gave her an easy excuse to avoid betraying her criminal family.

There are murders of mafia children even more heinous than that of Giuseppe. In 2015, in 'Ndrangheta country in Calabria, three-year-old Nicola "Coco" Campolongo was shot at point-blank range in the forehead along with his grandfather Giuseppe Iannicelli and his grandfather's twenty-seven-year-old Moroccan girlfriend.

Their bodies were found in a burned-out Fiat near the crime haven of Cosenza after Giuseppe had expanded his own drug enterprise into another 'Ndrangheta clan's territory and reportedly refused to give them a cut of a recent sale. A fifty-cent coin was found on the scorched hood of the car, a sign that the hit was about a debt, according to lead prosecutor Franco Giacomantonio.[4] "In all my years investigating organized-crime murders, none has been as horrific as this one," he told me on the sidelines of Coco's funeral, which was attended by local officials and even mentioned by Pope Francis. "It is unimaginable that a child can be made to pay for the crimes of his parents."

Coco was living with his grandfather because his twenty-four-year-old mother, Antonia Iannicelli, was in prison, serving a four-year sentence for the possession and sale of drugs. Police refused to let her attend her toddler's funeral, out of fear it could spark a gangland war if she showed up after rumors that she had cooperated with police to secure such a light sentence.

Italy's national police chief Alessandro Pansa signed an emergency proclamation in Coco's name to try to ensure the protection of mafia children. "We need to make sure the protocol does not forget children who are growing up in vulnerable situations outside the law, who may be victims or witnesses to crimes," he told me in an interview in 2015. "We need to make sure Coco is the last child ever killed like this."

Six months later, three-year-old Domenico Petruzzelli was caught in the cross fire in Puglia, where the remnants of the struggling Sacra Corona mafia have been clinging to power for years.

The toddler was sitting on the lap of his thirty-year-old mother, Carla Maria Fornari, who was in the passenger seat as her lover, forty-four-year-old Cosimo Orlando, drove the car. Her older children, aged six and seven, were in the back seat and dove to the floor when a car passing their vehicle opened fire, pumping twenty shots into the front seat at such close range they left paint from the shooter's car on the driver's side door as the bullets ricocheted.

Fornari, Orlando, and the baby were killed. The older children survived by playing dead after the car veered off the road and slammed into a tree. Those children were whisked to protective foster care far away from Puglia after authorities fully understood the dynamic of the crime. As survivors, they could have potentially described the shooters, thus their lives were in grave danger.

Orlando was murdered while out on parole after serving thirteen years for his role in the double homicide of a pair of twenty-year-olds in a drug dispute. The drive-by murder was classified by investigators as a vendetta for those murders, which had never been avenged. The baby's father, himself a convicted murderer, had also been gunned down in a mafia hit in 2011, meaning there was no one in little Domenico's immediate family who attended his funeral.

It is at times unfathomable to comprehend how a mother could take such risks when there is always an opportunity to go to authorities and live a protected life. The process is complex and not always assured, since evidence has to be corroborated before full protection can be granted. But when the alternative is a child caught in the cross fire of a vendetta, it is clear the bond and loyalty demanded by criminal groups is stronger than blood ties.

In 2014, Italian police tried to lift the lid on just what keeps people so loyal to such a deadly pact. They sent an informant to infiltrate a ritualistic 'Ndrangheta initiation taking place in the northern Italian town of Lecco, where the group has made substantial gains in recent years. The shocking video[5] shows men huddled around the new "devotee" in what feels something like a cross between a pagan ritual and a college fraternity initiation. The language is arcane, but the message is clear. Those being initiated must swear to kill themselves if they ever make a mistake and accidentally betray the organization. (If they do it intentionally, the other members will take care of his death for him.) The preferred choice of suicide is the cyanide pill they are told to always carry, or, if that doesn't work, a self-inflicted gunshot. "Always reserve one bullet," the man lording over the initiation says. "That one is for you."

"It is a mother's duty to inculcate in her children silence, gender differences, and contempt for public authorities, while simultaneously playing the role of a custodian of honor, keeping the flame of vengeance for offended men alive," writes sociologist Rossella Marzullo in her study of 'Ndrangheta children for the *Review of Social Sciences* in 2016. She says that within the 'Ndrangheta, children are incited to avenge the honor of fathers and brothers killed by the criminal groups they are part of. Trying to extract children from those toxic situations comes at a price—parents or family members who loved them when they were bad can no longer keep them close if they suddenly turn good. Schools have had limited success in trying to teach about organized crime when so many children are growing up in criminal families. Teachers can try to introduce concepts in the curriculum that illuminate what is really happening around them that might click with some children, but educators worry that it can also be dangerous. Teaching kids a different perspective on the culture in which they're growing up could upset the equilibrium at home and force them to drop out. If they get an education, at least they stand a chance. Those who don't will never escape their criminal destinies.

But the 'Ndrangheta group has recently seen a remarkable trend with a number of children forcibly removed from their family homes by the Juvenile Court of Reggio Calabria. There, judge Roberto Di Bella pioneered a program in which alleged membership in the 'Ndrangheta could be considered child abuse, punishable by the removal of the child from their parents—an about-face from writing off the future of these children through complacency. The effort started in 2002 when Di Bella got tired of seeing eleven- and twelve-year-olds hauled into court for acting as lookouts for their older brothers and fathers. Since then, he has removed around fifty boys and girls between the ages of twelve and sixteen from their families. In about one-fourth of those cases, the mothers choose to leave with their children, though rarely do they become state's witnesses.[6] In some cases, the men of the families insist the wives go along with the children to ensure they come back to the "family" once they are no longer minors.

Di Bella used legislation[7] based on the International Convention on the Rights of the Child, signed in 1989, and Italian Civil Code 315-bis to ensure children in Italy are "educated about the principles of legality, solidarity, human dignity, and alternative standpoints." But his real aim was to break the cycle of criminality that runs so deeply in 'Ndrangheta families, even though a worrying trend shows that taking the children away to be educated can backfire.

In an interview in 2019, just six years after the first kids were sent away, Di Bella told me that the new generation of highly educated daughters are actually coming back to their families and taking a more active role in drug trafficking, as accountants and sometimes even dealers. Having been educated abroad, they are often more tech savvy and culturally aware, which means they can help the criminal groups strategize on a more global level. In mafia families, women are rarely allowed to go to university. Prosecutor Cerreti explained to me that if children are educated or enlightened by meeting someone who cues them into the trap they are in, they will quickly see all that is wrong with the criminal world they live in and, most likely, get out of it. She has seen the success of the judge in Reggio Calabria take children away from criminal homes who don't go back. She has also seen this in some of her turncoats who saw the light and understood that all that they had learned from family members was wrong. As long as they are educated by the criminal family, there is less risk they will leave.

For the most part, that is why Pupetta stayed with the man she suspected of killing her first son. For all her fame and influence, she was conditioned to believe that she could not exist without him.

"I made mistakes when I was young," she said. "I stayed in relationships that were bad. I did it not for love but for necessity. Now women know better. Then we didn't." She said that she could not have easily afforded to take care of her twins without Umberto. And more than that, she wanted to be part of a family—a dream she thought had died when Pasqualone was murdered. Even though Umberto was hardly a good man, he made her feel part of something.

7

Drugs, Guns, and Vats of Acid

Debora took a risk—it could have been a trap—and scrib-bled a note on a grocery store receipt from her handbag and handed it to her. It read, "I will tell you everything to save my children."

Pupetta recoiled when I asked her if she had ever dissolved any-one in acid. "Don't be ridiculous," she said, as if shooting some-one more than twenty times is somehow a more civilized assassination. "Acid is for savages."

Pupetta's first murder was carried out with a handgun. The second—for which she was ultimately acquitted—was a decap-itation. Acid baths, while a mafia staple, are often reserved for extraordinary hits. The victim doesn't die right away, and in-stead their skin burns off in about fifteen minutes with, one might imagine, excruciating pain. After that, the organs and bones dissolve into the liquid, leaving no trace at all. The pain is exacerbated only by the practice of having someone who might also be under threat watch the whole ordeal.

Threats by visual example are common among all Italy's syndicates, and nowhere is this more evident than with the allies of the country's newest criminal gang, which has taken the use of acid as a deadly weapon to new heights. Despite the name, the Mafia Capitale, which is based in Rome, is not officially categorized as a "mafia" organization, meaning its criminals cannot be charged under Italy's special mafia laws, including Article 41-bis, which allows for "hard sentences" to try to get the perpetrators to turn state's evidence.

The Mafia Capitale is a loosely structured umbrella group that was run by Salvatore Buzzi and a one-eyed gangster named Massimo Carminati. Both were sentenced to twenty years in prison for mafia association, extortion, bribery, bid rigging, and false accounting related to the infiltration of the Rome city government in 2014. They reportedly received millions in kickbacks for fixing corrupt contracts in garbage collection, park maintenance, and refugee centers—the latter of which was, in Buzzi's words that were caught on a wiretap, "more lucrative than drug trafficking." In 2019, Italy's highest court ruled that Mafia Capitale is no mafia at all and just a conglomeration of clans that are not affiliated in ideology but more out of convenience. The court then abolished the sentences, and both criminally guilty men were released in 2020 with no strings attached, not even probation. In October 2020, Buzzi opened a burger joint in Rome with a mafia-themed menu, with burgers named after *Gomorra* and *Suburra*, which are the two most popular mafia-themed shows on Netflix in Europe. In interviews he gave before the opening, he said prosecutors pay double, judges pay triple, and anyone he was originally convicted with will get a discount.

The two most important clans that supported the Mafia Capitale's efforts were the Spada family from the coastal town of Ostia outside of Rome and the Casamonica family. Both are former Sinti nomad families, which Italians still refer to as zingari (Gypsies), who struck it big in the criminal world when the Casamonica patriarch, Vittorio, came to Italy's capital city. They run a business with an annual turnover of nearly $108 million, according to Rome police.

The last known boss of bosses of the Casamonica clan was a sixty-five-year-old woman named Gelsomina Di Silvio, who was arrested in 2019 and testified in a complicated trial that was sidelined and then restarted several times by the COVID-19 pandemic. Described as a "woman of character," and not in a good way, Gelsomina is unrepentant and wears her dark, wiry hair in a tight bun. She as closely resembles Pupetta as any crime woman does, constantly interrupting the court in her recent trial to say she regretted nothing. She was sentenced in June of 2020 to seventeen years in prison for mafia collusion, which she is appealing.

Gelsomina was widely thought to have been a turncoat, though in her testimony in the spring of 2020, she very specifically denied cooperation with authorities. "The news reports accused me of being a collaborator of justice and of having named my family," she testified, in part as a message to her family. "I am no stranger to these things. When did I ever mention someone's name? I have never reported anything to anyone. I have never been a collaborator of justice."

She is the second wife of Ferruccio Casamonica, one of the pillars of the Rome-based criminal family. She managed the clan's affairs even before her husband went to prison, and notoriously handed down punishments in person, including kicks, slaps, punches, knife wounds, and acid attacks.

Like Pupetta, she clings to her infamy, at times embracing it. From prison, she has written countless letters to the media, describing the crimes against her family and the "vendettas" carried out as a form of racism to their Sinti heritage. But she is cunning enough to know how to send hidden messages in these missives, and in early 2021 police asked the media not to print anything she sent out, since it very well could land them in trouble for collusion by publishing her coded prose. It is a classic example of Italian authorities being unable to stop the rot from the inside. The Casamonica family and its allies have killed people under horrific circumstances, according to numerous turncoats who worked on the periphery of the Casamonica family—often drug runners or lookouts who weren't bona fide family members and felt little allegiance to the group. There are never bodies to be found, because they were ground up and fed to animals or dissolved in acid. But to stop them, authorities must threaten the media from reporting what is happening under the noses of the public. It is a layered and complicated cycle that will continue to perpetuate until and unless the criminality can be stopped at its core.

In 2018, police finally started taking Mafia Capitale seriously and seized property in central Rome, including a posh seafood restaurant in the touristy area near Campo dei Fiori and a popular nightclub called Marilyn in the Testaccio district a few blocks from where I live. When they sequestered the spot, the local coffee bars were abuzz the next morning, with much whispering about who in the area might have been affiliated. Police also closed a beauty salon called Femme Fatale, where mobster molls helped launder money, and the Vulcano gym run by Domenico Spada, a former prizefighter who tied the two crime families together. Among the gym's valued patrons were five senators from Italy's then-ruling Five Star Movement.

Debora Cerroni is a thirty-four-year-old Italian beauty who was born into an almost certain life of crime in her own right before marrying into the Casamonicas. She very nearly died in a vat of acid poured by Gelsomina in one of the clan's creepy Roman basements in 2017. Cerroni is the first—and as of this writing only—female Casamonica turncoat, and the detail with which she has described the clan's complicated network has led to dozens of arrests and seizure of several million dollars in assets. "Gelsomina was in charge of us. She is evil, she commands, she is something out of the ordinary, she is the devil in person," Debora told prosecutors. "She needs to know everything, and be in charge of everything, everything, everything, everything! She is jealous of her children; she is the devil."

I interviewed Debora in a secret location in late 2018 just before she was sentenced to two years in prison for her own crimes, and she also struck me as someone very similar to Pupetta, a woman whose fate lay not so much in personal criminal ambition but was rooted in the circumstances of her birth—circumstances she eventually grew into. As we sat for the interview, which was arranged through the help of one of her lawyers at the time, I couldn't help but wonder how her life could have been different had she married into her own crime family, and not that of an emerging group.

Much like Pupetta's father, Debora's was a prominent gangster who never quite made it to the upper echelons. He was stuck in the hierarchy of the Banda della Magliana (Band of the Magliana), which was a mafia-style gang that had a successful track record in kidnapping, extortion, and murder. It was founded in 1975 in Rome and became best known for violent acts during Italy's bloody Years of Lead when national terrorism was carried out by extreme political groups. The Band wasn't necessarily political—they hired themselves out for all sorts of dirty jobs. But unlike Pupetta, Debora wanted out and, at least for the short term, collaborated with prosecutors who were able to make dozens of arrests based on her testimony.

The group was tied to Italy's traditional mafia groups, running drug and arms rackets in and around Rome for the Cosa Nostra, Camorra, and 'Ndrangheta. They often worked with all three groups at the same time without ever being fully recognized as true affiliates of any of them.

Debora's father was a specialist in extortion, and she says growing up she often overheard terrifying stories he told her mother after they thought the children had gone to bed. Debora told me that she had thought many times about turning her father in, but that she was sure her own parents would have killed her if she had turned on them.

The Band of Magliana was famously linked to the neo-fascist

Nuclei Armata Rivoluzionari (Armed Revolutionary Nuclei), which was responsible for a 1980 massacre at a train station in Bologna that killed eighty-five people and injured more than two hundred. It's the same group with whom the one-eyed Mafia Capitale boss Massimo Carminati honed his criminal skills as a young member. Carminati was famously acquitted in the 1990s of being an accomplice to the 1979 murder of a journalist named Carmine Pecorelli. He won his freedom thanks to a deal he made with prosecutors who were trying former prime minister Giulio Andreotti for mafia collusion. Ample evidence showed that Andreotti wanted the journalist dead and had close ties to Carminati, but the charges didn't stick. The evidence used in Andreotti's trial against the mobster and the politician was given by Tommaso Buscetta, the turncoat tied to the corrupt forensic psychiatrist Pupetta and her lover Umberto were accused of decapitating.

Carminati and Andreotti handily beat the charges of killing the journalist with the help of one up-and-coming attorney by the name of Giulia Bongiorno, who would make history in orchestrating the defense that won the freedom of American student Amanda Knox and her erstwhile boyfriend Raffaele Sollecito in 2013. Carminati lost his left eye in a shoot-out while trying to escape across the Swiss border in 1981 after an arrest warrant was issued for him. He returned after the statute of limitations ran out.

The Band is also widely suspected to be involved in the 1983 kidnapping of Emanuela Orlandi, the fifteen-year-old daughter of a Vatican employee whose mysterious disappearance remains a favorite topic for conspiracy theorists in Italy. Among the many alternative theories of her disappearance is that she was kidnapped to be a sex slave for priests deep inside the hallowed walls of Vatican City. The group was also thought to be tied peripherally to the 1981 assassination attempt on Pope John Paul II by Turkish hit man Mehmet Ali Ağca.

Debora was born in 1984, just as the walls were closing in around her father. By then, the end to the Band of Magliana's criminal tenure was inevitable, but they carried out a few last sporadic acts in their dying days to cement their legacy. Debora grew up under the constant shadow of accusations against her father and his associates, and was taught not that he was innocent of such accusations, but that his criminal activity was justified.

Debora says she spent most of her early childhood visiting her father in jail or covering for him when he was in hiding. "I wanted to escape that criminality," she told me. "Even if it meant just going to a different criminal gang." Debora admits she couldn't fathom what living in a normal law-abiding family would be like. And she didn't feel she deserved a chance to find out. "There is no avoiding where we came from," she said. "When you are inside, you feel like there is no escape and when you finally do escape, you are constantly afraid they will come and kill you. There is no peace in either place."

By her early teens, Debora started moving in different circles from other mobster daughters, who dated the sons of what was left of her father's Band of Magliana gangs. By her late teens, she was dating members of the Casamonica family, whose criminality seemed familiar but whose Roma ancestry she found exotic.

In the 1990s, the Casamonicas were emerging as an aspiring criminal association in Rome under the leadership of Vittorio Casamonica, who in the 1960s had moved in from the southern Italian region of Molise, where he was raised in a nomadic Sinti family. Vittorio's parents had escaped Nazi Germany when Hitler's henchmen started an ethnic cleansing known as the Romani genocide, during which around half a million nomadic Roma people were killed. The Casamonica family found a home with other nomadic people in southern Italy. But as postwar poverty ravaged the region, there was little left for the community to live off, so the Casamonica family moved north.

Once in Rome, Vittorio easily found his footing. He taught himself to read, separating himself from many of his peers who had to rely on street crime to contribute to the family income. Vittorio wanted to do better. He attended school and soon enough he was a mini boss among a clan of misfits who would never fully integrate. But he didn't want to be an outsider, so he started to copy what the Italian boys at school did, from the way they wore their hair to the twang of their Roman dialect.

Before long, he was being "trained" under the criminal direction of Enrico "Renatino" De Pedis, the de facto king of the Band of Magliana who was looking to rebuild his empire. He thought Vittorio would prove useful because he spoke Italian well but could also communicate in the Sinti dialect, which few understood. He never imagined the boy who grew up in the nomadic camps under the bridges of Rome possessed the criminal acumen it would take to one day threaten him.

At the time, the Casamonica nomadic people were finding a role as foot soldiers for the larger criminal organizations, but

Vittorio dreamed of being a boss himself. Later, when his dream had been realized, he loved to sing Frank Sinatra's "My Way" in one of his many palatial houses in the suburbs of Rome, which is a scene that his grandchildren and nephews captured on video and shared on social media to such an extent the videos are now viral.[1]

De Pedis would eventually be buried in the Vatican's Sant'Apollinare Catholic Church run by Opus Dei in central Rome, where young Emanuela Orlandi was last seen after a music lesson. In 2012, as part of a futile search for the missing girl, his tomb was pried open to see whether her bones were buried with him. They were not, but several sets of other unidentified bones were found next to his. Vittorio was there when De Pedis was originally buried, and he was there again after the church refused to put his remains back in the original Sant'Apollinare tomb. He was eventually cremated and his ashes scattered at sea near Ostia.

Even as the Casamonica power base grew, they were ignored by most authorities. Not even the anti-mafia police appreciated their full potential, in part because they were still considered common criminals by the authorities, who were sure they were incapable of garnering the respect from the more established crime syndicates. But that lack of scrutiny allowed the Casamonica criminal organization to grow unchecked, and they eclipsed the Band of Magliana, which finally dissolved in the 1990s; by then most of their members were dead or rotting away in jail. The Casamonicas married Italians from other crime families to try to thin their Roma blood, and distanced themselves from the nomadic Sinti people. The latter were still living in makeshift camps in and around Rome, and were a target of right-wing leader Matteo Salvini, who took great pleasure personally bulldozing their encampments. But the Casamonicas still practice the paramichia rituals of their heritage, albeit under much more refined circumstances than their nomadic peers.

In 2002, Debora married Vittorio's nephew Massimiliano Casamonica in a Sinti ritual that tied her to him until death—which was loosely interpreted as his right to kill her if she strayed. She was just eighteen years old. Twelve years and three children later, Debora had decided to leave. Massimiliano was in prison on a drug-related conviction and Debora started frequenting nightclubs and swanky restaurants with Italian friends who had never understood why she had fallen in with the Casamonica clan.

Word reached her husband in jail that she was straying beyond Casamonica control, so Gelsomina sent in Debora's Sinti sisters-in-law Liliana and Antonietta, who kidnapped her and kept her inside a hidden chamber in one of the family's luxury Roman villas for forty days, threatening to dissolve her in the large vat of acid they kept in a secret basement room.

When they finally let her out, it was on the condition she would remain faithful to the family. She tried to reach out to her family and old friends once more, but her former female in-laws took her back down to the basement and made her dip her hair into the acid. She remembers the smell and the sizzle, which she said reminded her of the burning flesh she had smelled wafting up from the basement years earlier. Until that moment, she hadn't realized what the strange smell was.

Debora says the vat drained into the same pipe as the villa's toilets and drains, meaning victims of the Casamonica clan were flushed into Rome's ancient sewer system.

Her imprisonment finally ended after she convinced the in-laws that she would stay true to her husband. But the first chance she got, she ran away and filed for divorce. She also filed a police report, but then changed her mind and refused to sign it out of fear of retaliation against her children, whom she had left in the clutches of the Casamonicas. The clan soon found her in a safe house her lawyer had set up, and they dragged her back to their Roman stronghold, where she says the Sinti sisters beat and tortured her once again. They spared her life only because her husband wanted to deal the final blow for her betrayal when he got out of prison. They threatened to kill her children if she ever tried to escape again, which put an end to her attempts.

In 2016, she attended the funeral of the godfather Vittorio, who had died of cancer at age sixty-five. A gilded hearse was pulled by six black stallions through central Rome beneath a helicopter that dropped rose petals over the procession. The police blocked traffic through the capital as the procession wended its way along the streets.

A lone trumpeter played Nino Rota's "Speak Softly, Love"—the theme from the *Godfather* movies—as Vittorio's coffin was carried into the Church of San Giovanni Bosco. White roses adorned the portico and massive posters showing him with a halo over his head were taped up on the basilica walls. "You have conquered Rome, now you will conquer heaven," said one. "Vittorio Casamonica, King of Rome" read another. Once the coffin and immediate family, including Debora, were inside the church, the theme from Stanley Kubrick's *2001: A Space Odyssey* blared from speakers for no apparent reason other than to underscore the surrealism of it all. Hundreds of people attended, including many nomadic Sintis who lined the perimeter around the church and cried that the son who did them all so proud had died so young.

Vittorio's funeral was a show of power by the Casamonica clan—and it managed to embarrass Rome's city leaders, most of whom were at the beach for the summer holidays when the spectacle took place. Meetings were called and questions were asked as the funeral ran across all the news outlets. Who gave the criminal family permission to fly a helicopter over Rome's normally closed airspace? Who authorized the police to provide protection and traffic control? No one seemed to know. The priest who conducted the Mass said the family were important patrons in the community. He admitted to me in an interview that he had baptized and married hundreds of members of the clan right there in the sizable Roman church that had tax-free status, thanks to the Vatican's immense influence over city politics.

Anti-mafia officials were both embarrassed and dismayed that such an important crime family could host what amounted to a state funeral in the heart of Rome. They justified their own scandalous oversight by saying that the Casamonica family was unimportant and only on the margins of criminality. But privately, they feared that they had simply overlooked what had somehow become one of the most powerful crime families in Italy. The Casamonica clan was under moderate surveillance, but at least part of the reason they remained unchecked for so long was because they spoke in a Sinti dialect and the Rome authorities just didn't have a translator who understood it.

At the funeral, Debora was secretly approached by a woman who whispered to her that she was an undercover police officer who had infiltrated the clan by posing as the Italian girlfriend of one of the Casamonica cousins. She had learned of Debora's harsh treatment because it was used as an example to threaten her, a warning that any "outsiders" would be watched extra carefully or end up like Debora. The officer told her she knew of the report she filed and, even though she wasn't specifically working Debora's case, would help her if she could.

It could have been a trap, especially since the police officer admitted being tied to a Casamonica man. Debora took a risk and scribbled a note on a grocery store receipt from her handbag and handed it to her. It read, "I will tell you everything to save my children." Her risk changed the path of the Casamonica family forever.

Within weeks of the funeral, Debora was able to escape the Casamonica clan thanks to the undercover cop. She arranged to get another agent to pose as one of the private drivers Debora had asked to have drive them to the prison for the weekly visitation with her husband. He was continuing to threaten to kill her, even though she had seemingly come around and decided to stay with him. At the very least, she was certain cruel beatings for her original betrayal awaited her, and their visits were a toxic mix of love and hate.

Once she and her children were safe in protective custody, she told investigators everything she knew, including addresses, names, and secret meeting places where the Casamonica clan met. She told them about the vat of acid and the many people who were taken into the basement, never to emerge from it.

From her safe house, she wrote a longer note to her rescuers. One translated excerpt in court documents reads:

> I always fight for my children, but I would like to guarantee them a future because unfortunately my life has given me that disease, which may also be one that I will never be cured of. My life is limited and you have helped me to take back the children and have arrested those beasts who exist without respect, who are ignorant, disrespectful to others (and I ask myself how I chose to choose to be part of them) and for this I will always be indebted. But maybe I can translate all that you want or teach you their language, or if I cover everything I have told you and that I have yet to tell you when you come here, I can testify against them . . . even if the risk against my life will rise . . . I can tell you these things because having lived and co-existed with them all this time I not only have to find the dignity of being a mother (as I really wanted for my children) but also to be a woman and to be an honest person, as I really feel I am. My children will have to follow different examples.

Debora later testified in a Bologna court about the inner workings of the organization, which was far more entrenched with the major syndicates in Italy than previously realized.

She also explained how the women of the Casamonica clan did all of the work: They made the decisions, paid bills with money hidden around their homes. The family spent thousands on reconstructive surgery for those who were hiding from the law and needed to change their appearances, or for women whose men didn't like the way they were aging. The Casamonica women also paid skilled lawyers who helped them fight small charges that might lead to bigger discoveries.

Debora described how the Casamonica women ordered hits, hid illicit drugs, and called the shots when it came to deciding who would get loans and how much interest they would have to pay, which, at times, topped 1,000 percent interest. They managed bodyguards who trained in the villas' private gyms in martial arts, and they decided which weapons would be carried and by whom, though the preference was always to be able to do bodily harm with fists and clubs rather than firearms, which are easily traceable in Italy. Debora was also trained in these criminal managerial skill sets, but she told police she never felt she could adequately play the role even though she grew up watching her mother fulfill a similar one for her own criminal father.

Thanks to Debora's secret note and testimony, which led to the escape of two other non-Sinti women married into the Casamonicas, multiple arrests were made in the summer of 2018, a full two years after Vittorio's funeral, which was the amount of time it took investigators to complete their investigation and corroborate Debora's leads. Meanwhile, Debora was in hiding and her own family disowned her for betraying an affiliate crime family.

By the time the last of the 2018 arrests were made, thirty-one people were in prison and three remained on the run. Police sequestered the beauty parlor that Debora told them about, where women who orchestrated criminal activity while getting pedicures or their roots touched up were able to talk without fear of being bugged. Debora also told them the address of the gym that was favored by local politicians and where Casamonica men trained in martial arts. Police shuttered restaurants in Rome's posh Parioli district and near the Pantheon, and a nightclub in the popular Bohemian neighborhood of Testaccio that was used for laundering money.

But the most surprising discoveries were made in the many lavish homes the Casamonica family members kept in slummy suburbs in Rome, which helped keep up the nomadic zingari facade. Police confiscated luxury cars, as well as hundreds of expensive Rolexes, thousands of euros in cash, guns, untold kilos of cocaine, jewels, and records outlining their businesses hidden inside gaudy furniture meant to look like faux-Baroque antiques. There were gilded or mirrored ceilings in the bathrooms, and the houses all had posing porcelain tigers throughout—which, when broken open, actually revealed safes with keys to secret properties stashed with jewels and cash in case anyone needed to make a quick escape. All of the homes had security systems that watched who drove within a few blocks and who entered and left the houses. As of this writing, police still aren't sure they have located all the properties tied to the clan, or how extensive the clan's reach had become.

Debora also tipped off police to a loan-sharking scheme run out of Ostia, where the powerful Spada crime family ruled the beachside resort town. Handwritten account books were found in the beauty parlor where the Casamonica women met, showing how loans of €10,000 were suddenly worth €600,000 and paid in cash, jewelry, drugs, and blood.

In 2017, a Casamonica family associate of the Spada family beat up a TV reporter live on the air when he was investigating whether there was an affiliation between the Mafia Capitale, the Casamonica family, and Italy's major criminal groups. At the time, dozens of other journalists came forward to say they, too, had been threatened or beaten when they tried investigating these connections, which the Casamonica family insisted did not exist. Court documents would later reveal that the criminal families kept special billy clubs dedicated to the beating of specific reporters. Previously, authorities had worked on the theory that the Spada family in Ostia worked only with the Mafia Capitale group, but they soon learned that both groups were tied together by the Casamonica clan.

The beating of the reporter caught on camera depicted the bloody side of the Casamonicas, and Debora's testimony underscored that such violence was par for the course. Her depositions included details of watching people being beaten to death in the family homes—in front of young children, who cheered and booed like the emperors during gladiator fights in the Colosseum.

After the initial arrests in July, police finally admitted openly the power of the Casamonica clan. "The family Casamonica has taken things to a new level," a police statement read. "Forging close ties with the Calabrian 'Ndrangheta and the Camorra of Campania, it has a total turnover of about €40 million a year."

Debora now lives outside of Italy with her sons, who have all assumed new identities. But she is sure she will one day be discovered and dragged back to the basement. So was Pupetta. When I told her what I knew about Debora and asked what she thought, she said, "The woman is doomed. You cannot leave a group like that alive, and in many ways it is better not to try."

Pupetta wondered why Debora would have given up a comfortable life, why she had to get away. "There are ways to gain power in an organization like that," she said. "She threw a real opportunity to be someone away."

Pupetta's infamy is in many ways what comforted her in her old age. When she died, she was celebrated as one of the most important "mafia women" in Italy, legendary for her crimes and misdemeanors, and an inspiration to those following in her footsteps. When I asked her about what legacy she wants to leave, she said simply: "That I fought for justice."

8

The Sin of Confession

Rita spent her childhood stuffing heroin into shampoo bottles and hiding cocaine in the side panels of cars on her mother's orders.

While the depth of women's true involvement in mafia organizations may be up for debate, their ability to persuade their loved ones against becoming turncoats and breaking the omertà is undisputed.

Pupetta never forgave Umberto for betraying her trust after he was arrested in 1993 during a sting operation in Peru. He swiftly confessed, becoming a pentito. In doing so, he joined the loathed ranks of mafia turncoats, like his former associate Tommaso Buscetta, who in many ways kneecapped the Sicilian Cosa Nostra with his spilling of secrets. In a letter to a mob boss in 2019, Pupetta blamed the pentiti for ruining her, implying that she was still part of some aspect of the criminal world. Otherwise, how could a confession by someone collaborating with law enforcement have any impact on her? In 2021, another revelation surfaced during a Camorra investigation into a money-laundering racket in which large sums of cash were paid to Pupetta for undefined services. By then, her daughter, Antonella, had made it more than clear that I couldn't contact her mother anymore. That she was still part of the criminal underground when I visited her house before the pandemic and yet denied being part of it underscored everything I thought about her and so many of the women in this book: that they are beyond rehabilitation, either so tied to the criminal world they have no way to escape, or they simply like it.

That suspicion would be proven correct when she died and the local police prohibited a public funeral. It is common for local police to prohibit mafia-tied men from being honored in death, but Pupetta was the first mafia woman to receive such a dubious honor. No other wife, mother, or daughter has been deemed so involved in organized crime as to have their funeral canceled.

When Umberto became a witness for the state, the Camorra swiftly murdered his brother Antonio and would have likely come after Pupetta and the twins if she had not already publicly cut ties with him.

Umberto's testimony led to forty arrests in and around Naples. He is very likely still alive, living under Italy's witness-protection program—which means he could be anywhere in the world. He had controlled the Camorra's South American cocaine route and had few direct ties to the tightly knit clans in Naples, which made his jump from perpetrator to pentito considerably easier since he wasn't in daily contact with other clansmen who might sense that he was under pressure—and threaten him if they sensed he might collaborate with authorities.

Pupetta swore she never once tried to get in touch with him after he left her to serve Dr. Semerari's murder sentence alone. But police records from his own testimonies show otherwise, outlining the many times that Pupetta did indeed reach out to him in various ways when news spread that he had turned. She never asked to join him, nor did she ask him to offer her protection. She asked only if he was sure he knew what he was doing, and to think about the many lives his testimony would destroy.

During Umberto's numerous post-pentito media interviews, he admitted to murdering and decapitating Semerari. In his most recently published interview, given to *La Repubblica* in 2017,[1] he was asked if he carried out the killing personally, to which he responded, "I cut off his head." The interviewer asked why. Umberto replied, with an irony apparent to everyone but him, it seemed: "He was a traitor, and whoever makes an agreement and does not keep it is a traitor. We are talking about a criminal arena, aren't we?"

In an interesting twist, he had told investigators that Pupetta had nothing at all to do with Semerari's death, though they were never sure if he was telling the truth or attempting to clear her name as a bid for forgiveness. When asked in the 2017 interview what went wrong between them, he told a far different story than she did. "I was gone a lot," he said. "Ultimately I went to South America. I met another woman with whom I had three children."

Pupetta, who physically bristled at any mention of that

interview and Umberto's nonchalance about having children with someone else, told me that there was no "greater scum" than a turncoat. I wondered if she was in fact hiding her personal pain behind the less personal betrayals. It was hard to understand if her hatred stemmed from him testifying against the criminal group they so prospered in—or if it was really because he killed her son and cheated on her. As I got to know Pupetta, I tended to think she truly was angrier over the criminal betrayal than the personal one, having taught herself at an early age not to dwell on emotional pain. "In any walk of life, betrayal is unforgivable," she told me. "It would have been better for him to commit suicide than to ruin the lives of so many people by confessing."

During my conversations with Pupetta, I asked her about the lives that the Camorra has ruined, the many murders and destruction of livelihoods that the criminal enterprise carries out even today. But like all those who believe in their syndicates, Pupetta truly did not see the irony of her anger at the turncoats for ruining Camorra livelihoods. She believed in the moral integrity of everything she had done and blamed any judgment of her lifestyle on misconception—not fact—despite the thousands of organized-crime members currently rotting away in prison and thousands more of their victims buried in family tombs or never to be found again because they were literally flushed down drains along with the acid they melted into.

Pupetta's disdain for pentiti is echoed by many mafia mavens. None so much as Giuseppina "Giusy" Spadaro and Angela Marino, the wives of Cosa Nostra boss Pasquale Di Filippo and his brother Emanuele, who together turned state's evidence in 1995 against the Sicilian mob. The brothers were arrested and facing charges for murder, among the many crimes that would have easily landed them in jail for the rest of their lives. Giusy and Angela were interviewed for potential involvement as well, but it was just a formality.

During one of the questioning sessions, a detective told Giusy that her husband had decided to break the omertà and cooperate with police, offering her protection and an opportunity to safely join him under a new identity in another country. Giusy instead called Italy's ANSA news agency and gave a scathing interview, in which she called Pasquale her "ex-husband" and detailed how she believed that he and his brother were disgusting. "We disown them," she said. "Better to have dead men than pentiti. For us, the bastard pentiti don't exist anymore."

The Di Filippo brothers' mother, Marianna Bruno, also publicly disowned her sons, as did their sister Agata, calling them in other interviews "vile things wreaking tragedy."[2] The women of the family then carried out what amounted to mourning rituals, closing themselves up behind the heavy shutters of the family home in Corleone and wearing black when they went out, which was only for Mass, acting as if the men had died and not just done what for many was the right thing. So deep was the wound for Agata, whose own identity was tied to being an integral part of a successful criminal family, that she attempted suicide. In the end Giusy, however, turned state's evidence and now lives under protection.

One of the most prolific pentiti in Sicily was Giuseppe Laudani who, at seventeen, was destined to take over a Cosa Nostra cosche, or clan, after his father's brutal assassination at the end of 2015. Giuseppe's father was murdered by rivals within the Cosa Nostra and his corpse fed to stray dogs; DNA from his gnawed bones was used to identify his remains some months after he disappeared. But instead of embracing the opportunity left in his father's wake, or even the urge to avenge his father's death, the younger Laudani went to the police to testify against the three women who raised him: Maria Scuderi, fifty-one, Concetta Scalisi, sixty, and Paola Torrisi, fifty-two, who he said were the real masterminds of the brutal and deadly Laudani gang. Concetta, his aunt, had been given the lead role after she was narrowly saved from an assassin's bullet by Giuseppe's father in the early 2000s. Giuseppe's father gave her and the other women—all with mafia pedigrees—the gift of raising his son. The three "queens of Caltagirone" were immediately tapped the mussi di ficurinia, "prickly pear–lip ladies," in what seems a mixed reference to both their personalities and facial hair.

Laudani's testimony spurred a massive raid in the Sicilian port of Catania in February 2016 when 500 heavily armed officers carried out arrest warrants for 109 people, including the prickly pear–lip ladies who ran the Laudani group for Giuseppe's father. The three were taken into custody for mafia association, extortion, drug trafficking, and illegal arms possession. Of the 109 people targeted by warrants, 80 were captured and 23 were already serving time. The remaining 6 are still at large at the time of this writing.

The information provided by the teenager led to the uncovering of a budding alliance between the Cosa Nostra factions near Catania and the cocaine smugglers of the 'Ndrangheta just across the Straits of Messina. He also told investigators how the group run by the prickly pear–lip ladies had acquired two bazooka rocket launchers to complement their considerable weapons cache, intended for killing anti-mafia magistrates. Police were able to corroborate his testimony with another informant, and the rocket launchers were located in a garage on the slopes of the often-erupting Mount Etna. A cache of weapons and ammunition was also found not far from the volcano's most active crater, which, had lava flowed in that direction, could have set off an incredible explosion.

The young man also testified against his brother Pippo and half brother Alberto Caruso, as well as his ninety-year-old grandfather, Sebastiano. While the haul was massive in terms of justice, it paid dividends in information as well. Laudani provided compelling details about how these three women wielded power and were far more sinister in their punishments and vendettas than many members of the group who had far more power and influence. The women referred to young Laudani as a "prince" who would become king, but in preparing him, they used a sort of tough love that included torture and what he described as borderline sexual assault.

His testimony was particularly harsh against the patriarch of the family, Sebastiano, who, he told investigators, "wanted to kill every enemy the family had." Laudani explained how the old man sent messages to underlings and foot soldiers through the family lawyer. "He has always commanded from prison," the grandson said.

Giuseppe Laudani is currently living under Italy's witness-protection program under an assumed name.

Such hatred for pentiti might at first seem like a contradiction. Women inside the mafia are often described as painfully loyal to their husbands, fathers, and brothers, following their orders and maintaining for the most part a submissive role unless empowered to do more. If those descriptions are truly accurate, it would be natural for them to automatically follow when their husbands disappear into witness protection.[3] But the fact that they are so offended by those who turn against the organization—which we are constantly told women are not allowed to officially join—suggests they are more than mere cheerleaders on the sidelines.

Having a husband side with the law also strips from them the prestige and protection they enjoyed as a mafia wife within their home communities. If a mafioso is killed or imprisoned, his wife maintains certain rights and honors and is taken care of by the organization. If the husbands or sons become turncoats, the women have to leave the organizations by default—organizations many such women played an integral role in expanding.

Farther south, in the depths of Calabria, the toe of Italy's boot and one of the country's most beautiful regions, the power that 'Ndrangheta women wield is the topic of fierce debate. Roles are still traditional, and local folklore suggests that men won't even allow their wives or lovers on top during sex because of a perceived allusion to female dominance. However, every woman—whether a turncoat, prosecutor, or mafia expert—to whom I ever posed the question of sexual positions and mafia affiliation found it a ridiculous legend that had little truth to it. Domestic violence rates in this part of Italy are among the highest in the nation, and rape is often used as a weapon between warring families. Punishing a rival by raping his daughter means she will never be able to marry beyond a certain level of criminal society.

There are fewer turncoats in the 'Ndrangheta than in the Neapolitan Camorra or Sicilian Cosa Nostra, in part because of Calabria's demonstrably corrupt legal system, which has seen its share of members inside the police forces tried for mafia collusion. Judges, too, tend not to stay in place very long in the local tribunals due to the threats on their lives, making it an uneasy environment to foster the sort of trust you need to get members of syndicates to turn.

Blood ties are also hard to break in the far south of the country, an area long forgotten by many national social programs, and where rampant poverty has left many with no choice but to join the superrich criminal group. This phenomenon is especially prevalent in Calabria, where women in general have a less prominent role in society. In the deeply traditional families of this region, daughters, mothers, and sisters exist in such close proximity to whatever business their sons, fathers, and brothers are involved in, there's little chance they don't assume a critical role in it. Given that so few opportunities exist outside these crime families, there is never a choice for them not to be directly involved.

One such shining example is Maria Serraino, a member of one of the 'Ndrangheta's most successful crime families.[4] She spearheaded their cigarette-smuggling business in Milan, where they controlled the criminally infested area around Piazza Prealpi after moving there from Reggio Calabria in the south during the 1960s. She took on the traditional Italian criminal family matron role behind closed doors, raising her sons to be skilled car thieves and international drug barons, which was easier in the wealthier north of Italy. But she was also the boss of the clan outside the home, too, managing the 'ndrina's affairs with the quick wit and finely honed skill of a seasoned criminal.

Eventually her own daughter Rita, who has been mentioned earlier in this book, turned against her after the young woman was arrested with a thousand doses of ecstasy she had been forced to smuggle for the family business. Rita spent her childhood stuffing heroin into shampoo bottles and hiding cocaine in the side panels of cars on her mother's orders. She told police everything: how her mother was the true boss of the clan, even though everyone assumed the group answered to her brother Emilio, who was based in Spain to run drug-smuggling corridors from Morocco to England and from Colombia to Milan.

"She's got it right there in her blood, in her veins," Rita told police, according to court transcripts. "My mother had all the power, because if she decided some job shouldn't be done, then the job wasn't done."

Rita spoke with mafia expert Ombretta Ingrascì about women's "hidden but substantial power in Calabria," describing one of her aunts as a "general in a skirt." Rita said her aunt was as bad as her mom, and "capable of killing a person with her bare hands."[5]

Among the many nicknames Rita said her mother answered to were Nonna Eroina, "Grandma Heroin," and La Signora, "The Lady." Another of the daughters' husbands, also a turncoat, testified that Grandma Heroin ran the drug enterprise with an iron fist, even ordering the murder of a key smuggler who was trying to set up a freelance drug trade on the side. Ingrasci's work to unpack Grandma Heroin's reign of influence uncovered a series of tapped phone transcripts, including one between the matriarch and her son Antonio in which she warns him that she's about to kill his brother Emilio, the presumed boss, if he doesn't bring in more money from Morocco. "Don't fuck with me. If I cancel out Emilio, for me he is done for, because I am already pissed off," she said, essentially threatening that her own child is expendable if he steps out of line.

Grandma Heroin also ran an arms trade, procuring weapons from easily corruptible police and running them to her dealers, often personally. She died in 2017 while serving a life sentence for murder and mafia association.

Not all daughters who want out of their criminal families leave as successfully as Rita, who was able to never look back after collaborating with police. In 2012, Italian weekly magazine *L'Espresso*[6] ran a horrifying exposé about the triangle of 'Ndrangheta territory near the infamous Gioia Tauro port, a massive harbor outside Reggio Calabria on the Tyrrhenian coast through which everything from drugs to stolen antiquities passes.[7] The area around it is thick with thieves who pilfer the spoils that come from the port. An estimated 2.5 tons of cocaine pass through the port each year. I have visited the port for a number of stories, including in 2019 when some of that stash of cocaine was smuggled in 144 crates of underripe bananas. The port is poorly controlled, with holes in the perimeter fences through which smugglers' vehicles easily come and go. Side streets lead up to access points and people are milling around on both sides of the fence. Those in uniform are easily as corrupted as those without.

Gioia Tauro is also the epicenter of honor killings, and the *L'Espresso* article paints a gruesome picture, highlighting twenty deaths in the span of just a few years. Some of the young women who were killed were caught engaging in romantic relationships online rather than dating from the local pool of criminals. One was the widow of a prestigious boss; she had started dating again without permission. Several had died by "suicide," often forced to shoot themselves or put the noose around their own necks and jump off chairs at gunpoint.

The main source of the exposé was Giuseppina "Giusy" Pesce, whose story has been told earlier and whose family remains among the deadliest in all of the 'Ndrangheta circuit. Giusy had once brandished a knife to protect her husband after he was shot early in their courtship, which won him over. But as her husband was drifting in and out of jail, Giusy, at the age of thirty-four, became the 'Ndrangheta's first woman to become a witness for the state. In Giusy's case, she escaped, but her three children, ages fifteen, nine, and five, paid a terrible price in the form of torture, starvation, and violence as a ploy to get her to change her mind and return home.

The idea was to brainwash the children into believing that the abuse they endured was due to their "bad mother" and her choices to betray the family. They were fed only with eye droppers, which eventually caused the five-year-old to suffer developmental issues from malnutrition. The nine-year-old boy was habitually beaten up by the children of other 'Ndrangheta families, who all stood by and watched him get pummeled. And the fifteen-year-old daughter was forced to write her mother letters of anguish in an attempt to convince her to stop collaborating.

Giusy left the 'Ndrangheta's clutches with the help of the prosecutor Cerreti, but eventually succumbed to the torture of her children, pressure, and threats. In April 2011, Giusy publicly accused Cerreti and her team of malpractice and undue pressure to confess. That statement paved the way for Giusy to return to her family and reclaim her children from their torture chamber. It also allowed Giusy to collect more information about the clan, which she reported to police a few months later, after ensuring that her children were safe.

Among the many revelations Giusy shared with the investigators, which led to the arrests of seventy-six of her family members and their associates, was the mantra she had been taught all her life and which makes the 'Ndrangheta so successful at dissuading pentiti: "An 'Ndrangheta woman who repents is a stain that only a family member can wash with blood." Meaning that if she is ever caught, she will be killed for collaborating, and anyone close to her is vulnerable as well.

Collaboration is often even more deadly for those who stumble into a crime family unknowingly, as did the young grad student Rossella Casini, who disappeared without a trace in 1981. She grew up far away from the crime ambit of Italy's deep south in an affluent family palazzo in suburban Florence, where she was pursuing a degree in pedagogy in the Magisterium Faculty at the University of Florence, which was a fashionable way to get a theology degree in the late 1970s without actually joining a religious order. In 1977, Rossella met a dashing young economics student in Siena named Francesco Frisina when he moved into a room her family rented out. She was attracted to his dark good looks, which were a far cry from those of the boys she was meeting at the time, who were all headed for the priesthood. The two soon fell in love.

Rossella, of course, knew her new beau was from Calabria, but her mother recalls that they never once thought he was part of a crime family. This was before the advent of the Internet, when searching family histories or even spying on someone's social media were not yet possible. The two moved forward at a healthy pace and were soon planning a life together.

In the summer of 1979, Rossella traveled with Francesco to his hometown of Palmi on the coast of Calabria. She had never been south of Rome and found the trip exhilarating. She loved his family, too—until Francesco's father, Domenico, was assassinated by 'Ndrangheta hit men from a rival gang[8] during her visit. Rossella knew immediately that she was caught up in a bloody mafia war. Francesco pleaded with her to leave, but she stayed in Palmi while he sorted out the affairs of his father.

Rossella eventually returned to school in Florence but went down to Calabria on the weekend of December 9. At the end of the weekend she said good-bye to Francesco and headed back to Florence. A few hours into her journey, she had a feeling that something was not right and called Francesco's home. When he didn't answer, she called his friend, who reported that he had been shot in the head during a scuffle in which he had allegedly tried to kill a rival just a few hours after their romantic weekend had ended.

Rossella turned around and, upon seeing him bandaged up

in the hospital in Reggio Calabria, insisted her beloved be transferred from the rundown center where she was sure he would die to the neurosurgical ward at the prestigious Careggi Hospital in Florence.

While he recovered in the northern facility, Rossella went to work on him, trying to convince him to repent and cooperate with police, which he did in 1981, giving vivid details of the family feud of which he was an integral part. Rossella testified as well, sharing details she had gleaned of the family she had only just met.

Not long after Francesco—by then recovered from his injuries—started collaborating, a relative lured him to Turin and convinced him to recant all he had told the anti-mafia investigators in Florence, which he did before returning to Palmi.

Heartbroken, Rossella went to Palmi in hopes of rekindling their flame. She was never seen again. In 1994, some thirteen years later, a pentito named Vincenzo Lo Vecchio shed light on her disappearance. Lo Vecchio, who was living in Palmi when Rossella last traveled there, told investigators that he was part of a crew sent to do away with "the foreigner" for turning Francesco against his family. Rossella was kidnapped and raped by the group of men who then cut her up into little pieces and fed her to the fish in the waters off a tuna processing plant.

The pentito's confession led to the arrest of four people, including Francesco, who allegedly was in on the kidnapping, rape, and dismemberment, along with his sister Concetta. The trial started in 1997, more than sixteen years after Rossella disappeared. But after a series of delays that lasted nine years, all four were acquitted. Still, in February 2020, the city of Palmi named a street after Rossella and her community in Florence dedicated a park to her.

Francesco was arrested in Rome in 2013, while he was allegedly working to expand the 'Ndrangheta's reach to the capital city.

When Pupetta spoke about organized crime, she mostly spoke of it as if it had nothing to do with her. She felt removed from it, not only because of her age, but because there is a sense of pride and territory among the groups. She was nicknamed Lady Camorra after committing her first murder, and she spoke of the two other major crime groups negatively.

The 'Ndrangheta, she said, are animals. The Cosa Nostra, she claimed, is impotent. The Camorra, she said, is not a criminal group at all.

"It is exaggerated by people like you," she told me early on. "You help perpetuate the myth of the mafia. It's your fault, not mine."

9

Dying to Escape

The pentito sent them to a field where police found more than a thousand tiny bone fragments and what was left of the necklace Lea was wearing when she went to Milan to meet Carlo.

In 2018, Pupetta agreed to be a guest on a local Italian TV program called *Reality Car*, which was sort of a talk-show version of James Corden's *Carpool Karaoke* without the singing. The host, Emilio D'Averio, dressed in a tuxedo on top, asks somewhat banal questions to mostly former celebrities while driving around the guest's hometown, which in Pupetta's case was Castellammare di Stabia.

When he asked her about the popular Italian TV series *Gomorrah*, she said she had to turn it off about halfway through the first episode. "*Gomorrah?* It is not educational," she told D'Averio. "Faced with all of those terrible scenes, I turned off the television and I never watched it again." She was particularly horrified about how children were cast as characters based on real-life kids whose horrific experiences with the Camorra she felt were "glamorized" and made to look like normal life. "Involving the children like that is unheard of," she insisted.

Many scenes in the series take place inside the Le Vele housing projects in the Neapolitan suburb of Scampia, which I visited for *Newsweek* in 2008.[1] One of the last of the condemned buildings was torn down in February 2020 as part of a revitalization plan for the crime-ridden Naples suburb. The seven apartment blocks shaped like sails were built in the 1960s and became symbolic of the Camorra's power. They were immediately taken over by drug dealers and criminals and the architecture, meant to mimic the narrow alleyways of Naples, became a perfect way to escape police when they dared to enter. In the 1980s, after a devastating earthquake left tens of thousands of people homeless, the complex became a shelter of sorts and squatters took over.

Rather than trying to clean up the debacle that Le Vele had become, authorities started tearing it down in 1997, as if getting rid of the structure would somehow get rid of the criminal system.

Visiting was a terrifying experience, though I wish I could go back. After my research for this book and my previous one took me deep into Camorra crime country where Nigerian women are trafficked, I could have entered that neighborhood with a greater understanding of the Camorra and without so much fear. At the time I visited Le Vele, I was the mother of six- and eight-year old little boys and admittedly earnest. Twelve years and two books later, I would approach the assignment differently, ask different questions, and be brave enough to want to see down more of the creepy, dark corridors. The city dismantled Le Vele during the pandemic, but the criminals by then had moved on.

I remember the sound of plastic syringes crunching like frozen snow under my feet when I walked up to the more inhabited of the two buildings. In the basement of one of the two buildings that still stood in 2008, women sitting behind folding tables sold single syringes of heroin for one euro apiece next to candy bars and cans of soda. Fix in hand, the customers would go down to the dark basement to shoot up. Patrons who pulled up in fancy cars were met by runners—mostly teenage boys— who exchanged wads of cash for brown paper bags.

The morning of the day I visited the complex with a photographer, there were around twenty cars in the parking lot and lines of people ran up the stairs from the basement around midday. A few hours later, the after-work crowd arrived and cars were double-parked. A queue of customers snaked around the outside of the buildings. Finished with school for the day, children rode their bikes over the syringes and played soccer, using the garbage as goal posts.

I was struck by how accessible this place was, that if I, an American journalist, could waltz up and start asking questions, surely police could shut the place down. But what *Gomorrah* so brilliantly portrayed was the extent of the integration the Camorra has in Neapolitan society, as do all the mafia groups in the broader Italian society. From a vantage point like Le Vele in 2008, it almost seemed the other way around, that the law-abiding society has integrated into the criminal world.

The photographer and I each had to pay a "fixer fee" of

€87.50 to our guide Lorenzo Lipurali, much as I paid Carmela to take me around to the ex-cons in Naples. Lorenzo's curiously specific fee was based on old Italian lire rates, and I was told in advance to bring the exact amount because Lorenzo wouldn't make change. Of course, the expectation was that most journalists would just round it up to €90 to give him a little tip, which I did.

Keeping our fixer happy seemed a wise investment, because for all intents and purposes, fees like his or Carmela's are protection money. A French TV crew visiting the complex the same day had refused to pay the protection fee, and they were held at gunpoint in one of the apartments until they paid the equivalent of five hundred dollars. Lorenzo talked on his cell phone to the men who were holding them and would report on the progress of their payment, perhaps as a lesson to me that I did the right thing by following their rules. I thought for sure he was making up the story until I heard about it on the news the next day after the French crew was released.

We sat in Lorenzo's immaculate apartment as his teenage daughter, who should have been in school, served espresso in little plastic cups. *Gomorrah* the film had just been released and was slated for an Oscar nomination for foreign film (which never ended up coming) and Lorenzo was excited. He slipped a bootlegged copy of the movie into a DVD player attached to a massive television. Electricity had long been shut off in the complex, so all the tenants had extension cords flung out windows and running to generators parked in a row near the entrance of the heroin basements. Lorenzo's TV cord snaked through a hole in the wall.

Lorenzo fast-forwarded to the part of the movie where he played a tenant trying to help neighbors maneuver a massive velvet sofa to one of the top floors. "There I am," he told me, pausing the disc to explain how hard it was to get the sofa to stop swinging. As he and the other men worked with the sofa, two preteen boys around the age of Lorenzo's daughter Anna philosophized about how they might have to kill each other one day since they were in different clans.

In Lorenzo's company, the photographer and I toured several apartments, almost all inhabited only by women and small children. The smell of bleach and cleaning products permeated the air and everything was spotless, even as it was falling apart. The windows that had bullet holes in them were scrubbed clean and the broken-down doors were polished to a shine. One woman named Maria Amaro invited me in for another cup of espresso, served in the same kind of plastic cup that Lorenzo used. Only later did I realize that it was because hot water was at a premium in the complex and doing dishes was a sure way to waste it, so almost everyone just used disposable dishes and cutlery. There was no official garbage pickup, so most people just threw their trash out of the windows into the courtyards below or down the elevator shafts. The elevator doors had been pried open but partially blocked with makeshift half walls to prevent anyone from falling to their death—unless it was intended they fall.

Maria liked the film, which she had also scored a bootleg of, but she was disappointed that the producers didn't show more of the "human side" of life in Le Vele. "People are afraid to come here," she told me as her three young daughters, all dressed in pretty pink tracksuits, rode new bikes up and down the corridors between apartments. "Everyone thinks we're going to kill them."

I asked her to describe what she meant, what the human element was that she felt was missing, and she said they didn't show any "normal life" and only focused on the crime. I asked her what normal life was like in Le Vele, and she described a recent torrential rainstorm. "I thought someone was throwing rocks down the roof or shooting," she said, pointing to the plastic roof over her small balcony. "But the rain was so strong the rats were falling off the roof like rocks." As I sat in her immaculate kitchen and sipped coffee I couldn't help but wonder how she thought stories like that would have softened the image in the film; how falling rats slamming onto corrugated plastic would seem "normal" to anyone.

Her neighbor Maria Mottola, another single mom with small kids running around, had an apartment just as spotless as Maria's. She also liked the film, but for different reasons. "The attention from the film isn't bad for us," she said. "The reality is much worse even than what they show, but maybe this is an embarrassment for the country."

Women in Le Vele are in many ways on the lowest rungs of the ladder for mafia women. They are not the wives and sisters of well-known capi, but rather the consorts of lesser-known criminals who end up taking the fall for bigger mobsters. These are the drug mules, the syringe sellers, and the runners who are unemployed and disenfranchised Neapolitans who possess no skills for legitimate work. They squat in condemned places like Le Vele, which often provide a cover for criminal operations like the heroin being sold out of the basement. But the "cash-iers" or men who come by every hour in fancy cars, entrusted by bigger mobsters to pick up the proceeds from the drugs sold here, would do nothing to protect their men running the busi-ness in Le Vele. These men on the ground are easily sacrificed in police raids, and the women in their communities are even more disposable.

Hundreds of women in mafia families have been brutally murdered over the years. Some die in unremarkable ways, ba-nally beaten to death by their husbands or wiped out in revenge attacks. The stories that tend to make headlines are the most horrific, like that of Lea Garofolo, who was killed—burned and buried—more than ten years after the first time she tried to leave the Calabrian 'Ndrangheta with her young daughter.

Although her father was brutally murdered when she was just eight months old, she was raised to believe that the crimes her family committed were justified and that wrong was actu-ally right. Lea was a classic southern Italian beauty with long wavy hair and an olive complexion. Her petite frame and larger-than-life energy seemed at odds, and drew friends to her.

But Lea didn't buy the idea that criminality was her destiny and from a very young age resisted the pressure to fit in. At the age of fifteen, she fell in love with a man named Carlo Cosco, who she believed was different because he lived in Milan, an-other planet from the dusty hills of Calabria. He seemed to be far out of reach of the criminal world she desperately dreamed of escaping. But what she didn't know when she agreed to elope was that Carlo worked for her brother Floriano, who led the family 'ndrina. Marrying Lea was meant only to help him climb the ladder. Lea was devastated. She became pregnant and tried to abort the pregnancy rather than raise a mafia child who could never escape. She became suicidal, but after giving birth to her daughter, Denise, in 1991, decided she had a reason to live.

Four years and several murders in her own backyard later, Lea went to the police and told them what she knew and took Denise away. Mother and child hid out in a convent in Bergamo for two years, but then got up the courage to first rent a small apartment in the small northern city and then a larger house. Lea worked odd jobs, Denise went to school, and life seemed normal. Lea even dated and made friends.

Then she made a mistake. She started going back to Calabria to see her family, whom she had theoretically betrayed. Lea wasn't a turncoat or pentita in the usual sense. Instead she had secretly testified against her husband and brother, and as such, she had never gone into hiding or entered the witness-protection program. But her real betrayal—at least to Carlo—was that she refused to visit him in prison, instead sending Denise with Carlo's brother Vito. Her absence sent the message that she was disrespecting him and, with it, the entire 'ndrina.[2]

Carlo started using his sway to terrify Lea, first by having someone set her car on fire to make sure she knew they knew she was living in Bergamo. When she was visiting her grandmother in Calabria in 2002, her brother Floriano slapped her in broad daylight in a public square and told her to go see Carlo in prison. Because he was family and this was Calabria, no one said a word. Two days later, the door of their grandmother's house where Lea and Denise were staying was torched to send the message that there was no escape.

Lea went to the Carabinieri the day her grandmother's door was set on fire and turned state's evidence, testifying about all she knew about everyone, including her brother, in exchange for protection for herself and Denise, which she thought would bring her peace and freedom. The police whisked her away to safety and moved the two of them every few months out of fear the 'Ndrangheta would kill them. Then, six years after she became a pentita, someone stalked and killed Floriano, first shooting him in the back and then ripping his face apart with gunshots, undoubtedly as a punishment for his sister's betrayal. At the same time, Lea started to rebel, growing tired of the confinement and venturing out without telling anyone, as was required as part of her protection. The state had not had luck prosecuting any of the claims Lea made, in part because there were no other pentiti to corroborate them, so they tried to kick Lea and Denise out of the protection program. She won an appeal to stay, but then left on her own a few months later.

In 2008, she entered the program again, but quickly left once more and spiraled between paranoia and depression for years. Finally, she reunited with Carlo—or so she thought—and reluctantly moved back to Calabria, where she depended on him financially. There, she was nearly kidnapped by a man disguised as a dishwasher repairman whose tool kit was filled with duct tape and wire instead of plumbing tools. Police suspected he was sent by an associate of Carlo's who didn't trust him to rein in his troublesome wife himself. Carlo paid for Lea's and Denise's apartment in Calabria and a smaller flat in Milan where she worked part-time under the condition that his mother and other relatives live with her. It was a hell from which she and Denise once again tried to escape. She did, but it would be her last taste of freedom.

In the summer of 2009, she reconciled romantically with Carlo against the advice of her lawyers and almost everyone who knew them both. On November 24, 2009, when they were supposed to rendezvous in the apartment in Milan to discuss Denise's future, she disappeared. A year later, a pentito told police that she had been brutally beaten in a Milanese apartment and her body burned for three days straight to destroy any trace. The pentito sent them to a field where police found more than a thousand tiny bone fragments and what was left of the necklace Lea was wearing when she had left for Milan to meet Carlo.

When Denise turned eighteen, she could make her own decisions about her life's path. She decided to testify against her father and others in a criminal trial that resulted in life sentences for six men, despite the defense's insistence that Lea was alive and well in Australia. Denise is now living under the same witness-protection program that failed her mother.

Over the ensuing years, memorials across the country have been set up in the memory of Lea Garofalo. Gardens, parks, and even streets in mafia towns have been named after her as a reminder of the pain and the price of justice and the overall failure of the state to protect her.

Not all turncoats fail to make a difference, and one of the most powerful in the history of the Sicilian Mafia was Giuseppina

"Giusy" Vitale, who became a pentita when she was in prison serving a term for a murder she had ordered as the head of a crime family. She was raised in a typical criminal family in Sicily in the 1970s, when widespread poverty pushed many young men into the criminal underground. Her brothers Vito and Leonardo ran the Palermo suburb of Partinico, where they grew up learning the type of violence that ensured their longevity in the mob. Giusy grew up under their control, often beaten and threatened and even forced to drop out of school at the age of thirteen so she wouldn't become smarter than they were.

Both brothers went into hiding and later ended up in prison with lengthy terms for murder, which left Giusy in charge. She first ran messages back and forth between their hideouts and later to and from their jail cells before eventually making her own often deadly managerial decisions. She was handed her own lengthy sentence for ordering her husband—a hit man—to kill a rival in 2003, which is when she decided to become a witness for the state.

While women's roles within the Cosa Nostra were especially hard to define, Giusy clearly got as close as she could to boss status. She had been a chief confidante of both of her brothers— who threatened her with death should she betray them—and only decided to testify against the cosca when she met another pentito by the name of Alfio Garozzo, who was allowed to visit her to try to get her to turn. The two fell in love, and Giusy's testimony provided colorful details that would have made *Godfather* author Mario Puzo proud, including witnessing a secret meeting in which superboss-in-hiding Bernardo "the Tractor" Provenzano was dressed in bishop's vestments and driven in a parish limo, which implied not only creativity on the part of the mob, but complicity on the part of the Church.

She was responsible for giving investigators vital details about Matteo Messina Denaro, the current Cosa Nostra boss of bosses, who was still on the run when this book went to print, but who may very soon be captured as those closest to him fall into various police traps. His fiancée at the time he disappeared was Franca Alagna, who competed for his attention with a number of lovers, including an Austrian woman who worked every summer at a tourist restaurant in Selinunte, Sicily, and with whom he is said to have fathered at least one child. But the child who made the biggest impression on authorities is Lorenza, the daughter he had with Franca and who is under constant surveillance, since police believe she and her father are, like most Italian fathers and daughters, extremely close. Every few months, Denaro's henchmen and mafia women are scooped up as authorities tighten the noose around him, but Franca, who lives with his mother, remains free. In October 2021, more than sixty people were arrested in an area of Sicily. Denaro was said to have been spotted in an SUV, but remains elusive to capture.

Giusy filed for divorce from her hit man husband, which is considered another unforgivable crime that calls for death, and her brothers have both vowed to kill her or send someone to do the job before they get out of prison. Giusy has remained defiant, speaking out through the press and insisting that she only testified to save her two children and marry Garozzo.

Not long after she collaborated, Garozzo rescinded his own testimony and removed himself from the witness-protection program, telling a judge that despite everything, "there is an indissoluble" love between the two. But that love may have been an arrangement of some sort to keep them both under the witness-protection program. Giusy told the court that Garozzo's collaboration was riddled with "falsehoods," charging that he had tried to set a trap for her with "false collaboration." And in fact, authorities had a difficult time corroborating any of what he told them, causing them to waste valuable time chasing dead ends when they could have easily been focused on a more truthful pentito.

To try to prove the point, court records show that he also described his lover Giusy as "certainly not a woman for whom a man can lose his head," implying that in appearance she was hardly the stuff of romantic dreams. Giusy has remained a collaborator and continues to testify in important criminal cases while living under protection, including her brothers' ongoing trial. She did, however, work to clear her ex-husband, Angelo Caleca, the father of her children, from the murder she was convicted of ordering.

Giusy's testimony was not only harmful to the Cosa Nostra; she also had plenty of dirt about the Italian security forces that allegedly helped keep Totò "the Beast" Riina on the lam for so long. Among the secrets she spilled were accusations against a top Carabinieri officer named Mario Mori, one of the arresting officers who eventually brought Riina to jail. Had Giusy not been there to witness this event herself, no one would have understood the complicity of these corrupt cops. She outlined how Mori had full responsibility of overseeing a known hideout

Riina used, and had once reported that there was no sign of the then-boss of bosses and didn't even search the villa—clearly to cover up what he really knew.

Giusy proved he knew plenty, testifying against even the police that documents Totò the Beast kept hidden away in that villa "if discovered, would have put a bomb under the state." She also told investigators that some of the Riina family hosted their patriarch and moved freely in and out of the villa under Mori's watch—or blind eye. Mori, who would have expected Giusy to protect him, was investigated for abetting mafia activity and later acquitted, having convinced the court that indeed he did not see any proof that Riina had been anywhere near the villa in question, despite Giusy's eyewitness accounts. Mori was tried again some years later for a drug-trafficking offense and eventually sentenced to twelve years in prison in April 2018 for threatening a judge.

In 2009, Giusy wrote a memoir with the help of Italian journalist Camilla Costanzo. The book, called *Ero Cosa Loro* (*I Was Their Thing*), clearly played off the Cosa Nostra name of the Sicilian Mafia; in it she recalls the day she decided to testify for the state. "My six-year-old asked me, 'Mamma, what is the mafia?' and that day I realized that there was still hope to save them."

Pupetta drew a blank when I asked her if she would live her life differently if she could. Not for one moment had it crossed her mind. "I had very nice things at one time," she recalled. "I had a house with a terrace in Sorrento, a beach house north of Naples. These were lovely places."

I had what was a guilty pleasure of visiting Pupetta's former summer home in the seaside town of Castel Volturno about half an hour north of Naples. It is an iconic 1950s-style bungalow surrounded by a high white wall that opens to an entrance with pillars on which diamond shapes have been cut. The square house has a curved stucco roof and floor-to-ceiling windows in the rooms that look out onto a long white wrought-iron arbor from which wisteria used to hang like silk. In the back, a patio with a portico-style ceiling like you normally see in Italian churches opens up to what was once an English-style garden with roses and short grass.

Pupetta's house was part of a wider development called Coppola Village built by Camorra-tied brothers. It was patterned on Miami Beach and intended to lure American soldiers who were stationed with Allied Forces Southern Europe in Naples (as part of NATO's continuing presence after the war), thinking they would like to buy weekend houses that felt like something from home. The project went bust before it was ever completed, and the buildings that weren't confiscated by the state went on to house mostly Camorristi who, like Pupetta, had invested early.

The idea for this Floridian neighborhood was hatched by the Coppola brothers Vincenzo and Cristoforo, apparently distant relatives of film director Francis Ford Coppola, whose roots extend from this part of Italy farther south. The brothers lost millions in the racket but made much of it back when their family company was given the state contract to tear some of the property down. Most of the larger buildings were brought down with TNT in the early 2000s at great expense to the state, all paid back to the family that caused the mess in the first place.

The US military refurbished and rented many of the high-rise buildings that weren't part of the state's sequester from the

Coppola family, who still owned them. The Americans gave up the last rental contract in the early 2000s, when paying money to crime families was no longer fashionable, thanks to greater awareness and anti-mafia investigations that started to home in on the curious financial relationship between the US government and the Neapolitan Camorra.

Pupetta was able to keep her house until it was confiscated by the state in the 1990s as part of a wider and somewhat inexplicable freezing of her assets. She lamented the loss. "It was a beautiful home, and right by the sea," she recalled. Inside, the floors were covered with hand-painted maroon and white tiles that gave the main rooms a feel of opulence and grandeur. A fireplace in the main sitting room was covered with colorful mosaics into which her initials, A.M., for Assunta Maresca, were embedded. The summer villa is now home to Alice's House, a cooperative for sex-trafficked Nigerian women, who have turned it into a sewing factory. The back garden, where Pupetta once hosted Camorra thugs, is now where the migrant women hold fashion shows and summer camp for kids.

A storage place that's under the floor in one of the back bedrooms was previously used to store contraband goods from cigarettes to heroin, police say. Now it's where the women run their own co-op where they store the colorful fabrics they use to make original designs.

Pupetta's sequestered house is symbolic of a hopeful change in the country. On the front, a sign states: "Here the Camorra has been defeated." Sadly, the sign is covered with graffiti and looks like someone tried to burn it. I showed Pupetta photos of the house, now largely unrecognizable, and most of her comments about the African influence and women who now work there are too vile to transcribe. Suffice it to say, she was severely disappointed that "such a wonderful house" had turned into what she described as a "whorehouse."

Even though Pupetta insisted she no longer had anything to do with her criminal past, her legacy will always be as an integral part of one of the deadliest and most dangerous criminal organizations in the world. She was twice convicted of murder tied to the Camorra, and suspected on dozens of occasions of mafia involvement. Her father was a known criminal. Twice she had children with known Camorristi. Her son has been arrested on suspicion of mafia involvement. Even well past age eighty, she never distanced herself completely from the underworld, and upon her death she was described as the first female mob boss.

It's a complicated mix of notoriety and fame. She is respected in so many circles as a woman who went beyond what was expected from her gender at the time. But she was a killer, even if the men she killed arguably deserved to die. Pupetta died in peace, feeling that she had no vendettas or debts to repay. Not many other women in the mafia will have such an easy time. "I sleep easily at night," she once told me. "I have no fear of dying."

10

A Few Good Women

"The mafia is a world based on deception and lies. I continued to live in the lie because I was forced into a double identity and a life in a secret location. Today even the smallest lie weighs on me."

Pupetta will never be remembered as a good person, even as age had softened her tough exterior. Her bold lies and bloody crimes are unforgivable—and why would they be forgiven, since she felt no remorse for any of them at all. Women like Pupetta who bask in the spotlight and seem to take great pride in their notoriety have in so many ways made it easier for the other bad women to follow. That she lived freely despite her murder convictions and other allegations is not so much a testament to her own strength and will, but to the failure and weakness of the state that cannot seem to eradicate the deep roots of organized crime in Italy.

Twice I met her daughter, Antonella, and both experiences

were unnerving. She has hints of her mother's beauty but little of her charm, and instead comes across as a slightly bitter woman who envies her mother's fame. Antonella is not a mafia woman, as far as any police investigation shows. She has managed her mother's affairs for years, so if Pupetta had ever been found culpable, she could have been considered complicit. It is impossible to know if she would like to be as notorious as her mother or if she was rejected from having an organizational role, but it seems clear that if she were affiliated with a clan she would be a different person and her agenda would be clearer. She was her mother's gatekeeper until her death, and now she guards her legacy.

Her objective seems to be to keep her mother from doing anything for free. The first time we met, I was leaving Pupetta's apartment when Antonella walked in. She seemed annoyed when she saw my espresso cup on the table. As I gathered up my notebook and pen to leave, she asked me simple questions that seemed to have no real purpose: Where would I publish the piece; who would be reading it; and who else was I interviewing.

The second time we met, she seemed angry that I had come back without going through her and told me in no uncertain terms not to return. Her mother, a woman I had by then spent enough time with to have seen as willfully strong-minded, seemed almost afraid of her. She kept her head down when her daughter spoke. She looked away when I tried to make eye contact. In fact, nothing I knew of Pupetta through my interviews and her interaction with others made sense when she was with

Antonella, who made her immediately seem weak and frail. At that moment, I felt sorry for Pupetta, assuming her daughter had taken complete control of her life and affairs. But on further reflection, I wonder if it was an act on Pupetta's part—if she was playing the part of the frail, elderly mother to keep her daughter from suspecting how capable she still was, part of an effort to convince Antonella that she had given up her previous life.

Though not much is known about Antonella's very private life, she and Pupetta seemed to have long been close. The two ran cheap clothing stores in Naples and Castellammare di Stabia until they went out of business in 2005. Pupetta was the shop salesclerk, selling gaudy polyester tops and tight skirts for five to ten euros to people who would come in just to brag that they had bought clothes from Pupetta Maresca. Antonella had other work, but she ran the business side of the operation, and her name was on the tax records undoubtedly because authorities were keeping an eye on Pupetta for anything that looked like tax evasion or money laundering. The way the business was set up on paper, Pupetta worked for her daughter, though the money to start the business may well have come from Pupetta. The spotlight never found Antonella, despite her ongoing proximity to her famous mother.

My final interview with Pupetta was cut short by Antonella, who shooed me away one winter afternoon just a few minutes after I arrived. Her mother didn't argue, and in fact I felt at that moment she was probably relieved. Antonella had come to her rescue spontaneously, it seemed, but perhaps the two had hatched the plan to cut things off. "I think you are done with your research now," she told me, making it clear she was in charge. "I don't think you'll be back."

After that interview, I tried in vain to meet Antonella separately, but she would not agree, citing the second wave of the pandemic and various lockdowns that kept the region around Naples hard to reach. But I felt she didn't want to meet with me because she would have nothing to say, that maybe she knew nothing of her mother's dark past except what she read in press reports. The two were close, undoubtedly, but the fact that she exists in the public imagination only as "one of Pupetta's twins" is likely a painful reality. She grew up in a home that was beyond dysfunction, likely knowing that her father was suspected of killing her stepbrother and surely knowing that her mother was an admitted murderess. In the end, I could forgive her for being standoffish. The last time I heard from her was a simple text message in which she wrote "mamma è morta." I had planned to see her a week after the funeral at the cemetery in Castellammare di Stabia, where there were clandestine plans to have a prayer service to mark the week since Pupetta's death. But police again prohibited any such celebration of such a villainous life. I doubt I will ever hear from Antonella again.

It boggles the mind to look at the volumes written about the various syndicates, the convictions, turncoats, and murders, which seem, at times, like movie plots too bizarre to be believable. But the mafia in Italy is still very real. Thousands of Italians have died in mafia-related crimes that don't always entail outright murder. Tentacles in the construction industry have led to the collapse of buildings in earthquake zones. During the 2006 earthquake that devastated the town of L'Aquila near

Rome, the antiseismic certification for a local school had been forged by a mafia-tied company and the school collapsed. That the earthquake struck in the middle of the night was a stroke of enormous fortune for the hundreds of children who would surely have been killed had it happened during the day.

The mafia infiltration of the toxic-waste disposal business I've mentioned has led to poisonous wildfires and soaring cancer rates in certain mafia territories, not least around Mount Vesuvius. They have also killed thousands through the illegal drug trade, both by feeding addictions and flooding the market with often-lethal substances like unfiltered cocaine and heroin.

The COVID-19 pandemic has given Italy's crime syndicates even more strength. Italy's strict Draconian lockdown that strangled the economy starting in March 2020 was the first such attempt to mitigate the spread of the virus outside of China. And while it worked temporarily to bring the numbers of cases and deaths down, it led to the shuttering of countless businesses and left others struggling to survive. Almost immediately after the lockdown began, the interior ministry warned that Italy's organized crime groups were already cashing in, lending money to struggling businesses on terms that would be impossible to pay back.

Things have changed very little from when Pasqualone helped farmers get more money for their crops by strong-arming manufacturers and buyers. What became apparent during the pandemic is that many of the Italian companies that run into dead ends with the state or banks find themselves desperate enough to deal with crime syndicates. As happened after World War II, most of these companies missed out on government help because they either underreported profits or had employees working off the books to avoid paying taxes, which left them invisible when it comes to stimulus checks and other payments meant to reflect the real cost of the pandemic. And in a country like Italy, where cutting corners and shifty accounting has long meant that the official statistics rarely reflect reality, the pandemic increased the gender gap in society, where women tended to be the ones shepherding their children's virtual learning from home and standing in long, socially distanced lines at stores instead of earning incomes.

In the criminal society, lockdowns had the opposite effect, because traditionally female roles meant women still needed to leave their homes for groceries and other essentials, and so had an easier time moving around than the men, who had no excuse to go outside. There were several incidents during the lockdown of March through May 2020 in which police claim they were able to pinpoint mobsters on the lam because of the women taking them food and clothing. Again, as in the case of Bernardo Provenzano, who police say was outed by freshly ironed shirts delivered by his partner, blaming the women tied to men who were hiding from justice made it easy for the state to maintain secrecy around its surveillance techniques. But in reality, an anti-mafia investigator told me the real reason they were able to find so many mafiosi on the lam was because they were using their cell phones so often. Prior to the pandemic, it was harder to trace them as they moved among service areas. But because anyone who dared leave their home during lockdown risked being stopped by police, the criminals stayed put, and apparently spent a lot of their time online.

The mafia influence during the pandemic didn't apply only to bailing out businesses. Raffaele Cantone, an anti-mafia magistrate, says crime groups also used the so-called "shopping bag" welfare scheme in which various criminal groups handed out free groceries and paid utility bills for those who lost work during the lockdown. These gifts to people in no position to refuse them gained buy-in from the population for the group's other activities, Cantone says. "Winning over community consent is achieved not only through intimidation, but also by buying social control over their territory," the theory goes. In short, if the groups were making life easier in contrast to greater restrictions handed down by the government, the subliminal message would be that the mafia wasn't that bad after all.

And in many of the cases during the COVID-19 pandemic, it was the women in these criminal groups who became the front-line workers for the mobs as a way to build trust—the exploitation of gender stereotypes was at work once again, since it was easier for women to deliver these handouts without rousing suspicion. Italy's patriarchal values create the perfect circumstances under which the concept of women as caregivers is always acceptable, even if these apparent acts of generosity actually break the law and extend the reach of criminal power.

Down the road, those who received a handout in their time of need will likely be asked to hide weapons or shelter fugitives. In some cases, they might even be asked to provide a safehouse for mafiosi to hold meetings.

Details of how the mafia works behind the headlines are garnered from turncoat confessions like the one anti-mafia prosecutor Alessandra Cerreti got from Giusy Pesce and other bad women who have—at least for a time—turned their backs on the criminality that they grew up with. The ensuing investigation based on Giusy's testimonies and Cerreti's dogged persistence led to prison terms totaling six hundred years.

Cerreti grew up in northeastern Sicily, a short ferry ride across the Strait of Messina from Calabria, where she had watched the evolution of the 'Ndrangheta from a small-time criminal group to the international powerhouse it is today.

She proves an important point: that many Italians who grow up in the heart of mafia-ridden regions are either directly caught up in the criminality or actively fighting against it, because they have a much keener understanding of the true damage these syndicates inflict on their communities.

Cerreti was not born into a criminal family, like so many of the women she has convinced to do the right thing. "That the criminality is ingrained from such a young age is what makes it so hard to break through," she said.

As the 'Ndrangheta moved north, so did she, focusing the earlier part of her anti-mafia career on the infiltration of the 'Ndrangheta and Cosa Nostra into Italy's wealthier northern reaches from her base in Milan. She saw overlap with jihadis—in style if not ideology—in the way these groups prey on the disenfranchised and offer them meaning at times when it is otherwise hard to find.

In 2009, Cerreti filled in for an anti-mafia investigating magistrate at the court of Reggio Calabria, and in January 2010 she requested a transfer south to Calabria so she could embed with other investigators and learn more about the group she had set her sights on disbanding. She determined almost immediately that the key to chipping away at the criminal group was to turn the women into collaborators by convincing them that it would be the only way to save their children—but she had no idea how difficult and deadly that effort would eventually be.

Coercing a confession out of someone whose life and identity are so intertwined with the criminal underworld is daunting. Mafia women have been brainwashed since birth, and convincing them that there is an alternative way to live takes a special kind of persuasion. Cerreti told me that growing up in the area helped her tremendously when trying to make breakthroughs with these women because she understood the mentality and the lack of alternatives. Crippling poverty leads to idle hands, she says, which become ready soldiers for the mob.

Even though the 'Ndrangheta, Cosa Nostra, and even Camorra have spread their tentacles north, their power still lies fundamentally in the impoverished southern regions of Italy. These areas produce the greatest despair and, though rarely, stories of immense courage and hope. Piera Aiello's is the latter. As a fourteen-year-old growing up in rural Sicily in the 1980s, she met a local teen Nicolò Atria, who she did not know at the time was the son of top Cosa Nostra boss Vito Atria. The don loved Piera and decided that she should marry Nicolò, even though they were young. While Piera didn't quite understand her young boyfriend's status in the local community, she knew that he was not like other boys because of the respect he garnered from people much older than he was.

As Piera recounted the story to me in 2018, after she had won a parliamentary seat, she and Nicolò had a spat and she broke up with him, only to be visited at home by Vito, who told her, in no uncertain terms, that she would marry Nicolò or her parents would be killed. Piera had no choice so, at eighteen, the two wed.

Their marriage started badly, with bouts of Nicolò's temper leading to daily beatings. He forced Piera to wait tables in the pizzeria owned by his family—a family that changed greatly only eight days after they wed. Vito was killed by a hit man, leaving Nicolò more power and, with it, the drive to avenge his father's death. "He swore he would kill the men who killed his father," Piera remembered.

Nicolò soon wanted a son, but Piera was not in love, and she secretly took birth control pills to avoid pregnancy. When he found out, he beat her even more and made her go off the pill and repeatedly raped her until she became pregnant. Their daughter, Vita, which means life in Italian, was born shortly after Piera had failed the Italian state exam to become a police officer—a betrayal that angered Nicolò even more. How could she dare join what was then seen as the enemy while carrying his child? "If I found drugs, I threw them away and was often beaten for this," she said. "I was kicked in the belly and risked losing the baby when I was eight months pregnant. I was forced to learn to shoot, I was forced to keep weapons at home."

Then, on June 24, 1991, armed men stormed the pizzeria while Nicolò was there and pumped more than three pounds of ammunition into him, killing him immediately. "My face was covered with my husband's blood," she said. "I despised Nicolò, but I felt pity for him. He was just a boy, twenty-seven years old, and they killed him like an animal."

Piera went to the police the next day and turned herself in

with Nicolò's sister Rita, and the two went on to work with anti-mafia judge Paolo Borsellino as state's witnesses until he was killed by a car bomb in 1992. Rita committed suicide a week later, and Piera and her then four-year-old went into hiding under Italy's witness-protection program until 2018, when she surfaced to run for parliament for the Five Star Movement. She handily won, even though she did not show her face until she was elected. Once in office, she had full police protection and changed her name officially back to Piera Aiello.

While living under witness protection for twenty-eight years with her daughter Vita, she married and had three more daughters.

She eventually left the Five Star Movement, but remains an influential lawmaker with a different party. She has worked on anti-mafia legislation and works to improve the quality of life for many who live under witness protection, sometimes forgotten after they testify. "For years I have lived in a world of lies," she said. "Yes, because the mafia is a world based on deception and lies. I continued to live in the lie because I was forced into a double identity and a life in a secret location. Today even the smallest lie weighs on me."

Today she is president of the anti-mafia association named after Rita, which works to help women find the courage to leave crime families, risky as it is. For her courage, in 2019 Piera was named one of the top one hundred most influential women around the world by the BBC.

Not all heroes battling the mafia are on the inside. Letizia Battaglia is a red-haired Sicilian chain-smoking photojournalist in her eighties. She describes her archives of photo negatives documenting the mafia crimes she chased over the years as "full of blood." Now she dedicates much of her time to curating exhibits and talking about the harm the mafia has done to the country. I have interviewed her and seen her speak about her experiences in Rome and in Palermo, where she commands the same sort of respect that mafia women would. And each time we talk, she pulls back a little more of the curtain about what it was like to be a woman covering the bloodiest crimes in the history of the Sicilian Mafia during the 1970s and '80s. "The phone would ring, and I'd hop on my Vespa and go," she told me once. "I had no idea what I was in for, but I knew it would be bad."

From time to time, she was threatened after her pictures of perpetrators in court made the front page of the local newspapers, but mostly the mafia dons didn't take her very seriously, she says. "They weren't afraid of me with my little camera. I didn't seem threatening until it was too late."

After her career took off and her name started making the rounds, she would get calls from people whispering threats or be the victim of the occasional curious flat tire that she was sure was meant as a message. But mostly she didn't care and kept on documenting the criminals, taking their pictures as they arrived in court, or of the coffins and crying widows and mothers of the victims. But her photos also implicated politicians and businesspeople who showed up at crime scenes and mafia funerals. More than once, anti-mafia investigators subpoenaed her photos for their investigations.

"The women were never on the front line in the courtrooms, but they were always there, passing messages and giving secret looks," she said. She remembers being at one trial during which a number of men were on the dock but the real mafia business was being done in the courtroom gallery, where deals were made and alliances forged. Letizia says the men would look into the audience and give subtle signals, maybe a shrug of the left shoulder while looking down to their shoes. "The women knew exactly how to read the messages, and they would go out and maybe a day or two later, I'd have to shoot another murder."

Letizia believes the mafia has ruined the country. "We were like a country at war," she told me. "But it wasn't even a civil war. It was good against evil, and it was bloody."

She has little hope that the mafia will ever be eradicated in Italy. "It is such a part of society now," she says. "It is no longer just about shooting and killing, they have infiltrated the governments, the successful enterprises . . . you can't even tell the good guys from the bad anymore. At least before [when crimes were more blatant] it was easier."

Federica Angeli is a journalist covering the mafia for *La Repubblica* in Rome who has played a major role in breaking open the Casamonica family dealings. As a result, she is under a constant death threat and was given a full-time police escort in the summer of 2013, when police overheard the dangerous Spada crime family of Ostia making plans to kill her.

The plotting against the journalist only emboldened her, and Angeli feels confident that the power of the pen can protect her. She is a frequent commentator on Italian television and her scoops tend to set the pace for the rest of the Italian media on all things Casamonica and Spada. On her Twitter profile, she posts the latest threats she receives in her bio. "If you write, I will shoot you in the head," she wrote recently. "You will never win against us." She signed the threat, "the mafia of Ostia."

Federica's popular 2013 book, *A Mano Disarmata*, which translates roughly to *An Unarmed Hand*, was made into a film that is hauntingly honest. Federica is a married mother of two, which adds a layer of complexity to her challenges since she is adamant that the children live a normal life in safety. The film portrays Federica's struggle within her family, including tense times with her husband as he tries to talk her out of covering the mafia "for the safety of the children." She resisted and felt her life's calling was to dismantle the deadly group, which she testified against for the first time in 2018.

Her story is a compelling one, and as a woman, she has a certain empathy for the mafia women she covers, easily understanding the power struggles within the family dynamic as well as the professional structure.

Journalism in Italy, much like the mafia and the Church, showcases the worst of what patriarchal structures offer. Even Federica's own bosses at times told her that despite her unparalleled skill at storytelling, she might be better off giving it all up to stay home or risk ruining her marriage or robbing her children of their mother. She has resisted and remains one of the most important journalists covering the mafia, always aware that those who tell these stories are as disposable as the criminals their stories are about.

Other reporters have remained as steadfast as Angeli in refusing to be silenced. Maria Luisa Mastrogiovanni has reported on criminal gangs from Puglia. Her groundbreaking reporting on how the Sacra Corona infiltrated the local government resulted in multiple threats. It was never clear who—the criminal group or the corrupt local government—was trying to shut her up, but they threatened her young children while they were in school. Mastrogiovanni eventually left the region for her own safety and that of her family, though she continues to report on organized crime. "I've left my home in Casarano in order to protect my husband and my children, because I couldn't be sufficiently protected from a possible attack," she told Reporters Without Borders. "There are not enough police officers to combat the mafia and to defend the journalists who cover this subject."

Marilena Natale, who lives and reports from Caserta in the heart of Camorra country, was given a police escort after anti-mafia authorities overheard clansmen discussing ways to silence her. She kept the escort for a while but then ultimately gave it up, fearing that they, too, could die. "If the Camorra wants to kill me it is not fair that my bodyguards must also die with me," she told Women's News Network. "I didn't choose to be a journalist focused on crime news. The crime news chose me. When I started to investigate and I saw with my own eyes injustices, I couldn't stop myself to know more and give to my readers what I discovered."

There are more than a thousand Italy-based journalists who have received death threats from the country's various organized crime groups. Just 15 percent of those are women, which underscores the dominance of men in investigative journalism, often because editors overlook women out of fear they aren't up to the job. But the number of women who risk their lives to expose Italy's rotten underbelly is growing.

It is not by coincidence that this book on mafia women has only a few stand-out examples of a woman fighting the mob. The press is always eager to entertain the whims of "mafia women" and give them a platform to call out "unfair persecution" and "archaic laws" they blame for their legal trouble. It is enticing clickbait to write about these women, glamorizing their lives. The heroics of the rare female prosecutor or journalist who risks her life to fight the mob are considerably less sexy.

Time and again, Pupetta personally went to the press—even holding two press conferences to call out Raffaele Cutolo's NCO and another to stick up for her brother Ciro's innocence. During the latter, she appeared dressed in an overtly provocative getup—leather and fur—that she knew would hold the press's attention and guarantee her coverage, no matter what she said. Pupetta continued to understand both the allure of the "mafia woman" mystique and how to exploit it, especially for the media. After the short press conference in which she stood up for her brother—an accomplice in her first murder—she pandered to various journalists she hoped would write favorably about her. In the end, as she could have predicted, the press instead focused on what she wore and her oversexualized demeanor. Nevertheless, she made the front pages of all the Italian national papers then, and again when she died.

It is easy to blame mafia women for normalizing criminality and using society's recognized fascination and titillation with all things "mafia" to their advantage. But as I sit with all of the women I've interviewed, mesmerized by every detail they feed me, eagerly recounting each experience to anyone who will listen, I cannot help wondering who is truly at fault for romanticizing the mafia.

Shortly before her death, I reached out once again to Pupetta, hoping for one last meeting—one last hit of what had come to give me an incredible sensation of risk and excitement. She was nowhere to be found, the number I had used now suddenly dead. I called a police source to see where she might be, and she told me that last she heard Pupetta was in a casa di riposo, or nursing home, which made no sense given that in Italy children take care of their elderly parents. In fact, it wasn't true at all, just one more fabrication to fit the circumstances. The letter Pupetta wrote to ask for help in employing her son in the Camorra's businesses was now a central part of an investigation that clearly wouldn't have been easy to try if Pupetta was somehow deemed infirm. I imagined she instead went into hiding, perhaps on a terrace in Sorrento where she still owned a property.

But less than two months after I last tried to reach her, she died in her sleep at home. Wherever she had been, she drew her last breath in the apartment where I had come to know her. I wonder what clothes she was buried in. I would like to think someone had dressed her in a low-cut, animal-print blouse and choker, pulled her hair back, and set her mouth into a sort of *Mona Lisa* smile. I want to remember her that way. I am sure that is also how she would like to be remembered.

By few standards of measure could Pupetta be described as a good person. She was involved in a criminal industry that ruins thousands of lives each year. But she was smart, courageous in ways both good and bad, and an exceptional self-made woman loved by many in spite of her obvious flaws. She was incredibly loyal to the Camorra, a doting parent (if you don't count not avenging the murder of her son), a dutiful wife (if helping commit murder defines that), and a role model to hundreds of mafia women who have followed her. And even though I know that I should not, I can't help but admire how she—like many women in Italy—managed to find her way around all the obstacles in this male-driven society and come out on top.

Acknowledgments

The scourge of organized crime in my adopted country cannot be understated. Popular culture has romanticized the Italian mafia for decades, which has normalized a phenomenon that ruins lives and local economies every single day. This book does not seek to glamorize such criminality even as it explores the stories of women who have had no choice but to stay in crime families.

I thank first and foremost the women portrayed in this book who trusted me—to the extent they trust anyone—with their stories, as tragic as they are. These women who end up on the front lines of crime families are usually born or married into it. It has often been said the only way out of these families is in a police car or a coffin, and I will never underestimate the difficulty of these women's circumstances.

I thank Pupetta especially for allowing me a glimpse into her complicated world, complete with many cups of coffee and warm—if not often disturbingly dark—humor. I dreaded what she would think about this book as much as I looked forward to handing her a signed copy. That she would be the first mafia woman ever to be banned from having a public funeral proved to me that she was the right focus for a project such as this.

The hardest part about writing this book was how much I really liked all those I met. I often wonder who they would be had they not been born destined for a life of crime as much as I wonder how any of us would behave had we been born in their circumstances.

There are so many people I cannot thank by name due to the danger it would put them in, but this book could have never been written without the cooperation of various magistrates, police, lawyers, and advocates working on behalf of and against the unforgivable crimes of these mafia women.

I also thank Felia Allum and Clare Longrigg, who have both done amazing research on this topic. It paved the way for me to better understand so much before I started my own research.

This book would not be possible without the undying support of my agent and friend Vicki Satlow, with whom I spent hours and bottles of prosecco hashing over this project. Her belief in this book, her determination to see it to print, and her support in the writing process have been second to none.

Random House Canada editor Craig Pyette not only inspired me to write better, he also taught me so much about what makes a good book. His insightful, detailed attention to this project has made me a better writer on so many levels. I cannot thank him enough for his obsession with this topic and professionalism and for pushing me beyond what I could have done on my own. Thank you also to the amazing team at Penguin Random House for their enthusiasm, fabulous book cover, and constant support in making this project the best it can be.

Thank you to Erin Friar McDermott, my coconspirator, friend, and editor at *The Daily Beast*, who painstakingly went over this manuscript more than once to make it better and who never balked at my ridiculous questions. I am also forever indebted to my sister Sherri Latza Stekl, who read the manuscript so many times she must surely have it memorized, and whose brutal honesty has always served me so well. I trust no one's honest advice more than hers.

Thank you to my editors at *The Daily Beast*, who give me space to write about organized crime and who support me in my external projects, especially Katie Baker, Tracy Connor, Nico Hines, and my late friend Chris Dickey, who died far too soon in July 2020 and to whom this book is dedicated. And to my colleagues at CNN, who have always been supportive of my projects.

My sons, Nicholas and Matthew, have always worried about my work and rarely as much as with this project. I thank them for giving up so much of the time I should have spent with them to pursue my journalistic goals—not just now but throughout their whole lives. They have given more for the success of my career than anyone, and while I can never give them back the time, I am so proud of the young men they are.

And finally, I could never succeed in my professional dreams without such amazing personal friends including the Cocktail Philosophy Club members, my journalist friends, and the various sentimental companions in my life throughout this project who have all provided invaluable inspiration.

Reporting Notes

For the purpose of this book, "mafia women" refers primarily to daughters, sisters, mothers, and wives of mafia men. There are rare exceptions of women who enter into a criminal family who have not in some way grown up somehow affiliated with one.

I refer to all Italian organized-crime syndicates in this book as "mafia" organizations, crime syndicates, or criminal organizations interchangeably. By definition there is only one true Mafia and that is the Cosa Nostra in Sicily. But even Italy's judiciary uses the lowercase term "mafia" more generally, charging men and women across all groups with mafia-related crimes under the Article 41-bis law, which allows for life sentences for mafia offenses unless the criminal cooperates with authorities, becoming a turncoat or male pentito or female pentita. The law is under review after the European Court of Human Rights found it violated human rights, and Italy's own Constitutional Court found it unconstitutional.

The 'Ndrangheta (pronounced en-DRAN-get-ha) is based

farther south in Calabria at the toe of Italy's boot, and is made up of 'ndrina or 'ndrine (pronounced en-DREEN-ah or the plural en-DREEN-eh), which are groups that are often family based.

The Cosa Nostra, "Our Thing," is also referred to as the Sicilian Mafia and is the best known of Italy's groups. Based on the island of Sicily, it is run by a boss of bosses at the top of a pyramid structure who controls hierarchical levels of cosca, or family clans. It is tied to the main crime families in the United States, though the 'Ndrangheta has also recently infiltrated many countries including the United States, Canada, and Germany with great success.

The Mafia Capitale (Capital Mafia) in Rome is an unorganized cluster of criminals that, despite the name, the Italian judiciary does not yet recognize as a mafia group. As such, it cannot use mafia-related legislation against them, even though their crimes mirror the work of the other groups.

I also mention other criminal groups, including the Sacra Corona (or what's left of it), which is based in Puglia at the heel of Italy's boot on the Adriatic Coast; and there are other groups in Italy, including the Albanian mafia, which is present in southern Italy; the Chinese mafia, which is present in the garment industry in central Italy; and the Nigerian mafia, which works with the Camorra in the drug-smuggling sector.

There is no mafia #MeToo movement—women may be doing the killing and leading the clans, but they are still often victims of unthinkable domestic violence, sexual harassment, and exploitation. While they have reached levels of notoriety, even the most powerful women bosses have not yet reached true equality when it comes to respect, and perhaps never will. They can order a man to be killed, for instance, but they cannot divorce their husbands without being killed themselves.

This book focuses on the women who have been empowered within the male-dominated system and climbed the criminal ladder to the upper echelons of criminality. I have written here about women who found "success" within their corrupted family and societal structures, those who have found power in what is still very much a man's world—and, in most cases, have lived to tell about it or in other cases, died trying to get out of it.

Mafia expert and journalist Clare Longrigg wrote the First Testament of the mafia women's bible in her 1995 book *Mafia Women*,[1] in which she gave women the credit they deserved. Through her research, she exposed the females who climbed the criminal ladder and became forces to be reckoned with. Before that, mafia women weren't seriously studied outside of the academic realm and were often portrayed as caricatures created in the minds of men or written about as pure infotainment.

My own well-worn copy of Clare's book has served me well over the years, and she inspired me to revisit Pupetta, a much younger and more vibrant version of whom she interviewed in the 1990s, when the mob doyenne lived in sunny Sorrento. I ran into Clare at a Christmas party in the London suburb of Islington in 2019, a few months after she edited the *Guardian* Long Read excerpt of my book *Roadmap to Hell: Sex, Drugs and Guns on the Mafia Coast*, which documented the Nigerian women who are trafficked for sex in the heart of Neapolitan Camorra territory near Naples. Meeting her was like meeting any idol, and I was thrilled when she kindly agreed to read an early draft of this book.

Her reporting was the first to shine an international light on women in the mafia. She was also one of the first to bring mafia stories to English speakers, long before any had heard of Roberto Saviano or any of the journalists who followed the *Gomorrah* author.

I have used Felia Allum's three distinct periods of the evolution of mafia women as my guide. From the 1950s to the mid-1970s, Allum says women were primarily part of support systems in families and wider communities. From the mid-1970s through the early 1990s, they started defending their men in courts and elsewhere, often relying on the willing press to help spin their stories of corrupt judges and longstanding biases. From the early 1990s to today, women have become the actual criminals, taking part in everything from money laundering and white-collar crimes to murder and extortion.

This book does not have a happy ending. The mafia is responsible for the deaths of thousands of people every year either directly through homicidal acts or indirectly through the various trafficking entities and general corruption they have engaged in for so long. But this book will introduce you to the women who have earned respect in their particular field, and who will accept nothing less.

Notes

1. PUPETTA'S KITCHEN

1. Felia Allum, *The Invisible Camorra: Neapolitan Crime Families Across Europe* (Ithaca, NY: Cornell University Press, 2016).
2. Barbie Latza Nadeau, "Italy's Triangle of Death: Naples Residents Blame Child Cancer Rates on Mob Disposal of Toxic Chemicals," *The Daily Beast* (November 21, 2013, updated July 11, 2017), https://www.thedailybeast.com/italys-triangle-of-death-naples-residents-blame-child-cancer-rates-on-mob-disposal-of-toxic-chemicals.
3. Enrico Deaglio, *Patria 1978–2010* (Milan, Italy: Il Saggiatore SPA, 2010).
4. Allum, *The Invisible Camorra*.
5. Clare Longrigg, *Mafia Women* (London: Vintage, 1998).
6. "'Diletto per amore!' sostiene la difesa di Pupetta Maresca," *Corriere Della Sera* archive (April 4–5, 1959), https://archivio.corriere.it/Archivio/interface/view.shtml#!/MjovZXMvaXQvcmNzZGFoaWRhY2kxLoA3MDYiNw%3D%3D.
7. "Pupetta sotto l'acusa 'aggredisce' la corte," *Corriere Della Sera* archive (May 1959), https://archivio.corriere.it/Archivio/interface/view.shtml#!/MzovZXMvaXQvcmNzZGFoaWRhY2kxLoA2OTcoMw%3D%3D.

8. Paul Hofmann, "'Crimes of Honor' Debated by Italy; Trial of Woman in Naples for Murder of Husband's Rival Stirs Nation," *The New York Times* (April 7, 1959).

9. Italian Penal Code.

10. Barbie Latza Nadeau, "Coronavirus Puts Italy's Most Vicious Mobsters Back on the Street," *The Daily Beast* (April 24, 2020, updated April 30, 2020), https://www.thedailybeast.com/coronavirus-puts-italys-most-vicious-mobsters-back-on-the-street.

2. CRIME SCHOOL / NAPLES' NOTORIOUS PRISON

1. Felia Allum and Irene Marchi, "Analyzing the Role of Women in Italian Mafias: The Case of the Neapolitan Camorra," *Qualitative Sociology*, vol. 41 (2018): 361–380, https://doi.org/10.1007/s11133-018-9389-8.

2. Rosella Marzullo, "Mafia Children: From Future to Past. Knowing Other Realities to Learn Freedom," *Review of Social Studies (RoSS)*, vol. 3, no. 2 (Autumn 2016).

3. Ombretta Ingrasci, "Women in the 'Ndrangheta: The Serraino–Di Giovine Case," *Women and the Mafia: Female Roles in Organized Crime Structures*, ed. Giovanni Fiandaca (New York: Springer, 2010): 47–52.

4. Clare Longrigg, *Mafia Women* (London: Vintage, 1998).

3. THE STRONG AND THE SWEET

1. Barbie Latza Nadeau, "Family of Most Dangerous Mafia Turncoat Ever Comes Out of Hiding: 'Just a Call Would Kill Us All,'" *The Daily Beast* (June 15, 2019, updated June 16, 2019), https://www.thedailybeast.com/family-of-most-dangerous-mafia-turncoat-tommaso-buscetta-comes-out-of-hiding-just-a-call-would-kill-us-all.

2. John Dickie, *Blood Brotherhoods: A History of Italy's Three Mafia* (New York: PublicAffairs, 2014).

3. Felia Allum, "Doing It for Themselves or Standing in for Their Men? Women in the Neapolitan Camorra (1950–2003)," *Women and the Mafia: Female Roles in Organized Crime Structures*, ed. Giovanni Fiandaca (New York: Springer, 2010): 9–17.

4. Dickie, *Blood Brotherhoods*.

5. Barbie Latza Nadeau, "Mobster Madonnas: The Rise of Women in Sicily's Mafia," *The Daily Beast* (December 17, 2017), https://www.thedailybeast.com/mobster-madonnas-the-rise-of-women-in-sicilys-mafia?ref=author.

6. Barbie Latza Nadeau, *Roadmap to Hell: Sex, Drugs and Guns on the Mafia Coast* (London: Oneworld Publications, 2018).

7. "Poliziotte in bikini arrestano una capoclan della Camorra," *La Repubblica* (August 29, 2000), https://www.repubblica.it/online/cronaca/bossa/bossa/bossa.html.

4. SEX AND HONOR

1. "La Arcuri è Pupetta Maresca Quella vera: 'Ha la mia tempra,'" *Il Giornale di Vicenza Cultura* (June 4, 2013), https://www.ilgiornaledivicenza.it/home/cultura/la-arcuri-%C3%A8-pupetta-maresca-quella-vera-ha-la-mia-tempra-1.331057.

2. Franco Di Maria and Girolamo Lo Verso, "Women in Mafia Organizations," *Women and the Mafia: Female Roles in Organized Crime Structures*, ed. Giovanni Fiandaca (New York: Springer, 2010): 90.

3. Umberto Ursetta, *Vittime e Ribelli: donne di 'ndrangheta da Lea Garofalo a Giuseppina Pesce* (Cosenza, Italy: Luigi Pellegrini Editore, 2016).

4. Barbie Latza Nadeau, "Bunga-Bunga Nation: Berlusconi's Italy Hurts Women," *Newsweek* (November 15, 2010), https://www.newsweek.com/bunga-bunga-nation-berlusconis-italy-hurts-women-69733.

5. Claudio Finelli, "Gay nei clan, il racconto di Saviano: 'Per i boss sono una vergogna,'" *Arcigay* (November 16, 2016), https://www.arcigay.it/en/articoli/gay-nei-clan-il-racconto-di-saviano-per-i-boss-sono-una-vergogna/#.Ya5FslMo-Bs.

6. "Secondigliano, arrestato 'Ketty': il trans a capo degli scissionisti," *La Repubblica Napoli* (February 12, 2009), https://napoli.repubblica.it/dettaglio/secondigliano-arrestato-ketty:-il-trans-a-capo-degli-scissionisti/1589581.

7. "Bacio camorrista fuori alla questura," *Corriere del Mezzogiorno* (June 8, 2011, updated June 9, 2011), https://corrieredelmezzogiorno.corriere.it/napoli/notizie/cronaca/2011/8-giugno-2011/latitante-una-villa-camaldoliarrestato-reggente-clan-amato-190821145124.shtml.

5. 'TIL DEATH DO US PART

1. Barbie Latza Nadeau, "The Boss of Bosses Dies. Will Sicily's Mafia Turn to the U.S. for Leadership?" *The Daily Beast* (November 18, 2017, updated November 20, 2017), https://www.thedailybeast.com/the -boss-of-bosses-dies-will-sicilys-mafia-turn-to-the-us-for-leadership.

2. "Italian mafia boss Bernardo Provenzano, 83, dies in jail," BBC (July 13, 2016), https://www.bbc.com/news/world-europe-36782555.

3. Attilio Bolzoni and Francesco Viviano, "Mio marito capo dei capi? No, Provenzano Ã una vittima," *La Repubblica* (December 13, 2000), https://www.repubblica.it/online/cronaca/riina/provenzano /provenzano.html.

4. Lorenzo Bodrero, "The Rise and Fall of Mafia Women," *Organized Crime and Corruption Reporting Project* (April 26, 2019), https://www .occrp.org/en/blog/9642-the-rise-and-fall-of-mafia-women.

5. Bodrero, "The Rise and Fall of Mafia Women."

6. *Organized Crime and the Legal Economy: The Italian Case* (Torino, Italy: United Nations Interregional Crime and Justice Research Institute, 2016), http://unicri.it/sites/default/files/2021-06/UNICRI_Orga nized_Crime_and_Legal_Economy_report.pdf.

7. Felia Allum, "Doing It for Themselves or Standing in for Their Men? Women in the Neapolitan Camorra (1950–2003)," *Women and the Mafia: Female Roles in Organized Crime Structures*, ed. Giovanni Fiandaca (New York: Springer, 2010): 14.

8. Monica Massari and Cataldo Motta, "Women in the Sacra Corona Unita," *Women and the Mafia: Female Roles in Organized Crime Structures*, ed. Giovanni Fiandaca (New York: Springer, 2010): 63.

6. TOXIC PARENTS

1. Cecilia Anesi and Giulio Rubino, "For Love or Money: An 'Ndrangheta Daughter on West Africa's Cocaine Trail," *Organized Crime and Corruption Reporting Project* (November 13, 2017), https://www.occrp .org/en/28-ccwatch/cc-watch-indepth/7249-for-love-or-money -an-ndrangheta-daughter-on-west-africa-s-cocaine-trail.

2. Anesi and Rubino, "For Love or Money."

3. raytodd2017, "Global Web of Firms for Fraudsters Created by British Company Formations House," https://raytodd.blog/2019/12 /04/global-web-of-firms-for-fraudsters-created-by-british-company -formations-house/.

4. Barbie Nadeau and Sarah Aarthun, "'Unimaginable:' Italy mourns 3-Year-Old Killed in Suspected Mafia Hit," CNN (June 21, 2014), https://edition.cnn.com/2014/01/29/world/europe/italy-child-mafia -hit/index.html.

5. Euronews, "Mafia Initiation Ritual Caught on Tape: Chilling 'Poison' Oath," https://www.youtube.com/watch?v=Tod7Ct9_icE.

6. Gaia Pianigiani, "Breaking Up the Family as a Way to Break Up the Mob," *The New York Times* (February 10, 2017), https://www.nytimes .com/2017/02/10/world/europe/breaking-up-the-family-as-a-way -to-break-up-the-mob.html.

7. Italian Civil Code, Article. 315 bis.

7. DRUGS, GUNS, AND VATS OF ACID

1. La7 Attualità, "Vittorio Casamonica Canta 'My Way,'" https://www .youtube.com/watch?v=FLpjn9rLG80.

8. THE SIN OF CONFESSION

1. Elio Scribani, "Tagliai io la testa a Semerari aveva tradito un nostro accordo," *La Repubblica* (May 25, 2010), https://napoli.repubblica.it /cronaca/2010/05/25/news/boss_ammaturo-4312237/.

2. Anna Puglisi, *Donne, mafia e antimafia* (Trapani, Sicily: Di Girolamo Editore, 2012).

3. Robin Pickering-Iazzi, *The Mafia in Italian Lives and Literature: Life Sentences and Their Geographies* (Toronto: University of Toronto Press, 2015).

4. Beatrice Borromeo, "Parla 'Mamma eroina,' ergastolo per mafia: 'Portai io la 'ndrangheta al Nord,'" *Il Fatto Quotidiano* (March 6, 2015), https://www.ilfattoquotidiano.it/2015/03/06/parla-mamma -eroina-delle-prime-donne-lergastolo-per-mafia-ndrangheta-nord -portai/1483497/.

5. Ombretta Ingrascì, "Women in the 'Ndrangheta: The Serraino–Di Giovine Case," *Women and the Mafia: Female Roles in Organized Crime Structures*, ed. Giovanni Fiandaca (New York: Springer, 2010): 51.

6. Lirio Abbate, "Calabria, la strage delle donne," *L'Espresso* (July 24, 2012), https://espresso.repubblica.it/attualita/cronaca/2012/07/24/news/calabria-la-strage-delle-donne-1.45133.

7. Barbie Latza Nadeau, "Italian Mob Trades Weapons for Looted Art from ISIS in Libya," *The Daily Beast* (October 18, 2016, updated April 13, 2017), https://www.thedailybeast.com/italian-mob-trades-weapons-for-looted-art-from-isis-in-libya.

8. Natale Ciappina, "Palmi, storia d'amore e di 'Ndrangheta," *Magazine.it* (February 22, 2021), https://www.magzine.it/rossella-casini-40-anni-fa/.

9. DYING TO ESCAPE

1. Barbie Latza Nadeau, "Inside Europe's Heroin Capital," *Newsweek* (December 12, 2008), https://www.newsweek.com/inside-europes-heroin-capital-82831.

2. Testimony from Salvatore Cortese, turncoat who shared a cell with Carlo Cosco.

REPORTING NOTES

1. Clare Longrigg, *Mafia Women* (London: Vintage, 1998).